TRUMP 101

TRUMP 101

The Way to Success

DONALD J. TRUMP

with Meredith McIver

John Wiley & Sons, Inc.

ISBN-13: 978-0-470-04710-1

ISBN-10: 0-470-04710-0

Printed in the United States of America.

10 9 8 7 6 5 4 3 2

To my parents,
Mary and Fred Trump

CONTENTS

CONTENTS

Contents

CONTENTS

CONTENTS

CONTENTS

FOREWORD

Donald J. Trump has long enjoyed a high profile, but the popularity of *The Apprentice* has made him a genuine folk hero. In addition to running a wide range of thriving businesses, Mr. Trump is a symbol of the American dream, an icon of success, and an inspiration to millions throughout the world. The fact that he fought back to increase his empire and became a billionaire after being $9 billion in debt makes his story even more remarkable. Mr. Trump knows business from every perspective, every angle, up and down and inside out. In *Trump 101: The Way to Success*, he shares many of the practical principles that have guided his career.

EDUCATION—TRUMP UNIVERSITY

Mr. Trump is also dedicated to education. He considers it a major factor in his success and has made the decision to become an educator himself, through his public appearances, *The Apprentice*, his books, and now, Trump University.

I really feel that if you're successful, you have to give back, whether it's to charity, the community, or education. If you don't give back, you're never ever going to be fulfilled in life.

—Donald J. Trump

Trump University was founded to give businesspeople the critical skills required to achieve lasting success. Our exclusive educational products, services, courses, and programs offer world-class learning in concentrated, practical, and user-friendly offerings that fully leverage technology. Trump University programs come in a rich variety of learning formats including online courses, multimedia home study programs, live events, and audio courses. These convenient and success-oriented business programs are clear and easy to use, understand, and retain.

At Trump University, our students are entrepreneurs, professionals, and others who are not content with the status quo in their business career. Our faculty includes experts from the world's leading educational institutions, including Columbia University, Dartmouth College, and Northwestern University. Our teaching staff also includes Fortune 500 senior executives and outstanding entrepreneurs. Plus, Donald Trump's direct insights, experiences, and practical know-how guide you throughout.

Our team is dedicated to helping our students succeed in their business goals. Trump University is committed to the Trump approach of uncompromising quality in everything we deliver.

This Book

This book, which was developed through Trump University, is like a one-on-one conversation with one of the world's great entrepreneurs. *Trump 101: The Way to Success* is crammed with Mr. Trump's insights, stories, perspectives, and advice on how to succeed. It also gives you a glimpse into the Trump Organization and a detailed look at the 10-day period in his life when his son Barron was born.

We at Trump University are proud to bring you this marvelous book. And we are extremely grateful to Mr. Trump for sharing his insights. We wish you a long, happy, and successful career.

For more information about Trump University, see www.TrumpUniversity.com.

MICHAEL SEXTON
President, Trump University

New York City

Acknowledgments

I would like to thank my assistant Rhona Graff for her very professional help at all times, and Meredith McIver, my co-author, for being fast, responsible, and insightful. To Kacey Kennedy, thank you for the help with the photo coordination. All of you have made the job much easier for me.

To the fine people at Trump University, and especially the president, Michael Sexton, I would like to say thank you for a job well done. You've all contributed greatly to the smooth compilation of this book and I look forward to more collaborations with you.

To Mark Steisel—thank you for your excellent work and enthusiasm from the beginning of this project through its completion. Special thanks to Richard Narramore, senior editor, and Emily Conway, assistant editor, at John Wiley & Sons, Inc., for their fine work. Aidan Sinclair did a wonderful job on the cover design, as did Adam Eisenstat with his editing. Thanks to all of you. You've been a terrific team.

DONALD J. TRUMP

INTRODUCTION

I have a real passion for learning. It grew out of my days as a student at the Wharton School and my professional experience. My books and seminars have always included a strong educational or "lessons learned" slant. As I did more books and seminars and my television series *The Apprentice*, I saw that a lot of people really wanted to hear what I had to say. They wanted to know what made me successful and how they could benefit from my ideas and experiences.

At first, the groundswell of popular support took me by surprise. It shouldn't have, though, because the message has been there from the start: Education, research, and knowledge—learning in general—are at the core of my success. When people buy my books or show up to hear me speak, they're in effect doing the same thing I've always done myself—getting more information and education.

This book has been written to advance that same cause. It is a collection of my beliefs about business and life—my basic rules and principles. It also contains questions submitted to me on the Trump University blog and my answers. I'm sure that this information will help you have greater success and fulfillment in your business and career.

Another purpose of this book is to introduce you to Trump University, which grew out of my desire to impart the business knowledge I accumulated over the years and to find a practical, convenient way to teach success. Trump University doesn't just bear my name; I'm actively involved in it. I participated in creating the curricula, and my words, ideas, and image have been woven into the courses we provide.

I'm deeply and actively involved in Trump University because I firmly believe in the power of education and its function as an engine of success. It's virtually impossible to succeed without an education. I want to help people, and, simply put, the Trump University students want to be successful. I'm on their side.

Enjoy this book, learn from it, and have great business success!

DONALD J. TRUMP

New York City

1

DON'T WASTE YOUR LIFE ON WORK YOU DON'T LOVE

Passion will help you do better

I love real estate, making deals, building great projects, and hosting *The Apprentice*. Who wouldn't? My work puts me in touch with the most interesting and accomplished people. Since I love what I do, I do it vigorously and I do it better. Because I inject it with enthusiasm and passion, it doesn't feel like work. My passion spills over to everyone around me and motivates them to do their very best.

Luc d'Abadie, co-author with Les Hewitt and Andrew Hewitt of *The Power of Focus for College Students* (HCI, 2005), says:

> Somewhere between childhood and the real world one of two things happen, either you start to follow the dreams of your parents, your neighbor, or someone else, or you get caught up in

pursuing the dollars or status associated with a certain career. People who do this leave their passion on a shelf collecting dust and end up becoming part of the 70 percent of people who dislike what they do.

Passion is absolutely necessary to achieve any kind of long-lasting success. I know this from experience. If you don't have passion, everything you do will ultimately fizzle out or, at best, be mediocre. Is that how you want to live your life or a big chunk of it? You have to love what you do to fully devote yourself to it and to make it in a big-time way.

PASSION PROPELS

Passion motivates. Passionate people don't give up; their zeal eliminates fear. Since they love what they're doing, they don't want to stop. They come up with inventive ways to overcome obstacles that would stop others on the spot. Their passion creates an intangible, but powerful, momentum that can make them feel indomitable.

I've known people who had fantastic ideas, but who couldn't get the idea off the ground because they approached everything weakly. They thought that their ideas would somehow take off by themselves, or that just coming up with an idea was enough. Let me tell you something—it's not enough. It will never be enough. You have to put the idea into action. If you don't have the motivation and the enthusiasm, your great idea will simply sit on top of your desk or inside your head and go nowhere. Lack of passion is often the difference between failure and success.

INSIST ON PERFECTION

Passion can create business opportunities. I love to play golf, so I created Trump Golf, to build and operate world-class golf courses. Golf and business have similarities: both are brain games. You get out of them what you put in. Playing golf with business associates creates a relaxing atmosphere where everyone has fun. It gets them away from the office and into the sunshine and beauty of nature. That's why so many huge deals are closed on golf courses.

Through Trump Golf, I've found a lucrative way to combine my love for golf and business. We operate spectacular clubs in Westchester, New York; Bedminster, New Jersey; Los Angeles, California; Palm Beach, Florida; and Canouan Island, the Grenadines. These courses have given me extraordinary places to play golf and host friends and associates. Plus, my golf courses have been successful business ventures—which helps ease the pain of those putts I miss.

Trump National Golf Club, Briarcliff Manor, New York.
Photo courtesy of the Trump Organization.

3

 MAKE IT HAPPEN IN YOUR LIFE

Focus yourself on what you should be thinking about right now. If what you are thinking about is something you enjoy, you are on the right track for success.

- Track what you voluntarily do in your spare time. What you are always eager to learn more about and never find boring? What do you dream and think about when your mind drifts? Ask yourself:

  —What do you love doing?

  —What fascinates you?

  —What causes time to fly?

  —What makes you happy?

- Don't blindly pursue a career that others suggest or insist is right for you. It may be worth taking a pay cut for a job you love—and if you're an entrepreneur like me, it could make you a lot more money in the long run.

- See if any of your interests can be turned into a viable source of income. Talk to other people making money in an area you love. Could you do some variation of what they do or take it in a new direction? Do you have the training to get where they are? Can you get the training to do what they do?

- Don't begin a career solely for money or to please others, especially if it isn't what you love. Sooner or later, the money won't compensate you for the lack of passion you feel.

WARNING: PASSION CAN ALSO GET YOU INTO TROUBLE

Passion is a double-edged sword: it's a great motivator, but it can blind you and prevent you from seeing flaws that others can quickly spot. Overall, your passion is far more positive than negative, but you have to manage it so you can see the difference between right and wrong. I call it having *controlled passion*, which is a great asset.

My passion has occasionally gotten me in financial trouble. If you're psyched about a deal, you may go into it knowing that the market is going to turn down, but you're so passionate about it that you do it anyway. Sometimes it turns out poorly.

Get objective advice from individuals who care about you before doing anything you're really excited about—people who will be honest, objective, and open-minded. Take their advice seriously, even if it's not what you want to hear. Ultimately, the final decision of whether to proceed rests with you.

Ask Mr. Trump: Questions from Readers of the Trump University Blog

Q: What is it that gets you through the resistance to change and the resistance of organizations to look at problems that are relatively easy to fix?

DJT: Passion is the number one ingredient. It can overcome many difficulties and so-called impossibilities. Getting anything started requires passion. Your enthusiasm can convince others to go along and see things your way. Resistance can be good if it gets you to improve your idea. When someone can discourage you, you probably aren't determined enough. Be resolute. That's what it takes to get things done.

2

SET THE BAR HIGH

Make people ooh and aah

When I decided to develop properties in Manhattan, my father couldn't understand why. He had been successful in Brooklyn and Queens and thought that I should work there, too. However, moving into Manhattan was a long-standing goal of mine. Manhattan was the business, cultural, and social epicenter of the world; it was center stage and it was where I wanted to make my name.

Years later, after I successfully established myself in Manhattan and decided to build Trump Tower, I explained my vision to my father. I described the bold, beautiful, innovative glass and bronze exterior that would distinguish Trump Tower. Again he couldn't understand. Bricks had always worked for him, why not for me?

I explained to him that I wanted to set my own standard. I didn't want to build just another skyscraper; I wanted the most magnificent, dazzling, and admired show place in the world. Since this building was going to bear my name, it would represent me, so I wanted it to be exceptional, head and shoulders beyond anything that New Yorkers had seen.

When Trump Tower opened to rave reviews and quickly became a landmark, it was clear that my standard had been accepted, and in a big way.

My advisors suggested that I hang beautiful paintings in the lobby of Trump Tower. Although I love beautiful art, the idea seemed old fashioned and unoriginal to me. So I decided to install a waterfall instead. The waterfall is over 80 feet high and cost $2 million to build. It's absolutely spectacular and mesmerizing to watch. It has become a major attraction in New York City. In fact, it's attracted far more attention than if I had filled the lobby with the finest art.

Once again, I was creating my own standard and setting the bar high.

It's Contagious

Everyone has an opinion on what you should do and how you should do it. Although most people mean well and often offer sound advice, they don't necessarily know what's best for you. For me, a major joy of my business is being able to exercise my own vision and creativity and to express myself. I do it by developing bigger, bolder, more beautiful projects; ventures that have imagination, style, scope, depth, and scale—projects that make people ooh and aah and that deliver more than anyone expected.

How a business operates, the quality of the goods or services that it provides, starts at the top and radiates down through the entire organization. The people who work for me know that the positive, enthusiastic individual you see on television and in the media isn't a facade. I really am that way, from inside out. I have big ideas and the energy to follow them through. When people work with me, they quickly catch on; they realize that this is who I am and how I, and my organization, operate. My energy and positive attitude become contagious. People work enthusiastically, tirelessly, and determinedly and do terrific jobs. Everyone knows that the Trump Organization gets things done and that our projects are always first class. A big reason for this level of success is that I set a standard that everyone works to meet.

If you like to work hard, hard workers will want to work with you. The people who work with me enjoy the daily challenges and set their own high standards for their tasks. As they work, they constantly ask, "How can we accomplish more? How can we get to the top?"

Ask yourself, "What is the standard for which I want to be known?" Identify that standard and follow it. Don't shortchange yourself. Set the bar high!

—Donald J. Trump

 MAKE IT HAPPEN IN YOUR LIFE

Take the time to be thorough in whatever you undertake. Remain open to new ideas and influences. Remain fluid, not fixed, in your expectations.

- Find out who and what is the best in your field. Identify the trendsetters, leaders, and authorities. What are the reasons they're the best? Learn the standards they follow.

INSIST ON PERFECTION

When I decided to rebuild Wollman Rink in Central Park, I followed my own principles:

- Do the best job possible.
- Build as quickly as possible.
- Spend the least amount of money needed to meet your standards.

For seven years, New York City had been trying to rebuild and restore this beautiful skating rink, but it never seemed to work. I stepped in and finished it in three months and for less than 10 percent of the city's $21 million cost. Everyone benefited.

I set my standards for this particular project, worked according to those standards, and successfully completed the job. No, the restored rink didn't have a waterfall, it wasn't clad in bronze and glass, but it also wasn't rebuilt with bricks.

Skaters at Trump Wollman Rink.
Photo courtesy of the Trump Organization.

- Determine what you have to learn or do to become the best in your area of interest. Find ways to take classes, meet people, serve apprenticeships, and get the experience you need to accomplish your goals. Give yourself time to take it all in, to grow, and to learn it all thoroughly.

- Look for good ideas outside of your own areas of expertise. Find innovations, approaches, and practices that you could adapt for your field.

- In everything you take on, ask, "How can I make it better; how can I make a stronger statement; and how can I make it reflect better on me?" Then go out and do it.

3

THINK TRUMP SCALE

Bigger is better

Ilike to reach for the stars, and I want my projects to do the same. I'm constructing the two tallest residential towers in New Jersey that, not surprisingly, will bear the Trump name. Trump Plaza Jersey City is a $415 million condominium project that will include two towers, over 50 stories high, with 862 luxury condominiums.

The towers' positioning and design will provide striking views of the Manhattan skyline from nearly every apartment. Each building has a rooftop swimming pool, a business center, an 8,000-square-foot fitness center, an enclosed basketball court, and a private film theater. The towers may not reach the stars, but their residents will think they're in heaven!

Although I'm the largest developer in Manhattan, I decided to go across the Hudson River to Jersey City because I saw incredible potential there. I am good at predicting trends, and I think Jersey City has a big future . . . or I wouldn't be there.

Don't limit yourself. Think in what I call *Trump scale* and make a *big* statement. Don't build a single-family house without first seeing how much more it would take to make it into a

Rendering of Trump Plaza, Jersey City, New Jersey.
Photo courtesy of the Trump Organization.

multiunit building or even a development. Explore how to make everything you tackle bigger, better, bolder, and more exciting. Although you may not be in a position to realize your dreams now, you could be laying the groundwork for terrific future projects.

If you're going to be thinking, you might as well think big.

—Donald J. Trump

THINKING BIG STARTS IN YOUR MIND

Thinking small when you could think big limits you in all aspects of your life. People are capable of great things, but not if they don't envision themselves achieving greatness. Start with your own mind-set.

Remember the saying, "It's lonely at the top?" I don't agree with it. Someone who didn't want any competition probably coined it. I'm secure enough in my success to welcome competition, and being at the top is a great feeling. It is something you should definitely try. Thinking big can get you to the top.

It's Okay to Start Small

Start with small steps and work your way up by taking bigger and bigger steps. People like challenges. It's our nature. If you stay in sync with that premise, you'll build momentum and move forward in a natural, comfortable progression.

Think about the goals you want and the steps you need to achieve them:

- Do you have big or small plans?

- What is limiting or holding you back?

- How can you expand your vision of the future?

To move forward in a big way, concentrate on managing your future rather then dwelling in the past. Learn from the past, but don't stay there; it wastes time. Don't focus on old problems when you can look for solutions that will help you reach your current and future goals.

Einstein said imagination is more important than knowledge. Easy for a genius like Einstein to say, but he had a great point. Without imagination and the ability to think big, knowledge alone won't make you successful. Knowledge is a building block. Put imagination and knowledge together and in no time you'll have something big in your think-big tank.

 MAKE IT HAPPEN IN YOUR LIFE

You can develop an expansive mind-set that lets you paint in bigger, bolder, more colorful strokes:

- Before you start any venture, while it's still in the idea stage, imagine ways to increase its size, scale, or scope. Don't worry about being realistic or practical.

- Explore whether any of your ideas, or parts of them, could be achieved. Identify the hurdles that could stand in your way.

- Examine how to overcome those obstacles and the costs it would take. For example, should you bring in a partner to split the costs, risks, and returns or to provide the talent, expertise, or contacts you lack? Frequently, the time, effort, and expense of going bigger isn't much greater, but the rewards can be stratospherically more.

- If the timing for your expanded vision isn't right, the cost is too steep, or other problems are just too great, consider implementing parts of your ideas that you can achieve now. File the rest away because things always change, and what can't be done today could be a piece of cake tomorrow.

Ask Mr. Trump: Questions from Readers of the Trump University Blog

Q: What is the inspiration that keeps driving you, even after you have achieved more than almost anyone else on the planet?

DJT: I love what I'm doing. Because I'm driven by my passion for what I do, it's not work to me. At this point in my life, I don't have to work or make deals, but it's what I enjoy. The challenge is there, so why not meet it? To be truly successful, you have to love what you're doing. If you don't, the chances of success aren't great.

When I decided to build my first golf course, it was new territory for me: I had so much to learn. People wondered why I was doing it since I already had so many successful ventures in areas that were more familiar to me. I told them it was because I loved to golf, and I wanted to create spectacular courses to play on. I didn't need to build golf courses, but I wanted to—which was reason enough. Building the golf courses took a lot of patience and effort, but every minute has been worth it.

4

TOUGH IT OUT

Be persistent

Despite what some people think, I wasn't born with the Midas touch. I've been very lucky—I'm the first to admit and appreciate it—and I've had many advantages like a great education and fabulous parents. I'm also tough, determined, and persistent, and there's no way I would have become successful without these traits.

Being tough doesn't mean being nasty, difficult, or unreasonable. It means being tenacious and refusing to give in or give up. It means believing in yourself, in your ideas and projects, and being prepared to fight the good fight. It takes toughness to stand and fight for what you believe and what you want.

My battles have always fired me up; they've pushed me to do more than I originally thought possible. Ultimately, each battle has made me stronger.

Trump International Hotel & Tower, Las Vegas's tallest hotel, is now rising in the Nevada desert. Ironically, it will stand directly across the road from Wynn Las Vegas, the signature property of Steve Wynn. Steve, of course, is the longtime cock of the walk in Vegas and my one-time adversary. Steve reinvented the Strip with such mega resorts as the Mirage, Treasure Island, and Bellagio. Unlike someone else, Wynn Las Vegas is the first of Steve's projects to carry his name.

Steve Wynn and I go back to the 1980s when we squared off in Atlantic City. It was like the old Western standoff, "This town's not big enough for the both of us." We have always built big, and we have the egos to match. Many years and many buildings later, we're good friends. Steve is a great guy and a man after my own heart. He attended my wedding, and I'm no stranger to his social circle. Back in the 1980s, though, the competition was fierce.

SOME THINGS ARE WORTH WAITING FOR

Most people are impatient and want quick results, but waiting is often the smart way to go. It takes toughness to hang in there and wait, especially when you must wait a long time for what you want.

I waited 30 years to get Trump Place going—I bought the land in 1974. Thirty years is a long time to wait, but it was worth it. Right now, Trump Place is rising along the Hudson River on Manhattan's West Side, and it's the largest development ever approved by the New York City Planning Commission. It has changed the city skyline. As I write, we're more than halfway through, and when we're finished, Trump Place will include a

Trump Place.
Photo courtesy of the Trump Organization.

total of 16 buildings and turn former railroad yards into a fabulous residential complex. Most things don't happen overnight, and this is a prime example.

Things of value rarely come easy and usually require lots of preparation, time, and hard work. Along the way, people and events may derail you, slow you down, and get in your way. That's the reality of how business works.

THE LESSON OF MICHELANGELO

I once went to a lecture on creativity where the speaker said that creativity and tenacity go together and are essential ingredients for great accomplishment. The speaker asked, "What if Michelangelo had said, 'I don't do ceilings,' and walked away from painting the Sistine Chapel?"

It was an interesting thought, but painting a ceiling probably represented a creative challenge to Michelangelo. The Chapel was completed because Michelangelo was a tough, tenacious guy who never gave up; he had to be to paint those masterpieces while on his back.

Problems always pop up. Expect them. Being tough lets you work through them without becoming worn out or negative. Anticipating and preparing for problems will save you time and resources and stop surprises that could cost you a ton.

COURAGE

Refusing to give up takes courage. Courage is the opposite of fear; you can't allow fear to paralyze you.

Courage is resistance to fear, mastery of fear—not absence of fear.

—Mark Twain

Sometimes the most talented people fail and those who are far less talented succeed. Those who succeed move forward with confidence and never allow others to convince them to give up. In some areas, I don't accept excuses, and having courage is one of those areas.

After I bought 40 Wall Street, everyone advised me to convert it to a residential building, but I was convinced that it should remain an office building. Although these same people gave me all sorts of reasons and statistics, I wouldn't budge. I was right and 40

Wall Street has become a very desirable business address. Sometimes you have to be stubborn, stick to your guns, and not give in. Combine courage with passion and you'll achieve your goals, whether you're dealing with corporations or your own network.

 MAKE IT HAPPEN IN YOUR LIFE

Try these tips to toughen up:

- Become a planner. Examine every project in detail before you commit to it and plan every step you will have to take to make it succeed. Try to limit the surprises that will arise as the project proceeds. Don't dismiss any potential problem as too minor or unlikely.

- Realistically assess the greatest downside liability for each potential problem that you face. Price the cost of dealing with each in tomorrow's dollars and factor in the time and resources it could cost you.

- Build a financial cushion that will allow you to avoid being squeezed when problems and delays occur.

Describing my workweek has been one of my favorite parts of my books over the years, so I decided to include it in this book. It should give you an idea of how much I have on my plate in a typical business week.

Around mid-March of 2006, I started jotting down my daily activities for that week. Then, our baby, Barron William Trump, arrived a week early on March 20, so you will have to excuse me if every day isn't entirely precise. Barron's birth was so special that I decided to extend the week's notes to include it.

Donald J. Trump Speaking at Learning Annex Seminar.
Photo courtesy of The Learning Annex.

Few things are as exciting and schedule blowing as a new baby—just ask any father and he will agree—but Melania and Barron were very respectful of my travel schedule. I had been scheduled to speak in San Francisco with the Learning Annex on the original due date of March 26. Fortunately, Barron had different plans and arrived the week before, so I was home with Melania for this wonderful event in our lives. People often mention how positive and upbeat I am. Sometimes they think it's media hype, but I have a lot to be happy about!

A Very Special Week (Plus) in My Life . . .

Monday

8:30 A.M. Rhona comes in to go over my schedule, some contracts, and my travel schedule, which is looking pretty crazy this month. We also discuss my upcoming trip to Scotland in April and go over Mike Donovan's suggestions. Mike is my pilot and has been for the past 15 years. Rhona has been with me for 18 years and can be seen regularly on *The Apprentice* playing herself.

9:15 A.M. Bernt Lembcke, who manages the Mar-a-Lago Club in Palm Beach, calls to discuss the upcoming Elton John concert at Mar-a-Lago. Needless to say, Elton John is incomparable, and this event is completely sold out. On March 17, the St. Jude Charity Ball is at Mar-a-Lago.

Donald J. Trump with Elton John.
Photo courtesy of the Trump Organization.

9:30 A.M. I return some calls—one to confirm the Katie Couric charity event at the Waldorf, a Motown night featuring some incredible talent to benefit colon cancer.

I also return Brian Baudreau's call; Brian is overseeing my new tower going up in Las Vegas, and I'm pleased to see he's up and at it, seeing as it's only 7:30 A.M. in Nevada. Las Vegas is an incredible place, and the Trump International Hotel & Tower will be a gleaming addition to it.

10:00 A.M. I ask Bernie Diamond, executive vice president and general counsel, to come in. We discuss our joint venture with Phil Ruffin in Las Vegas and the status of the second 1,200-unit tower to go up there. The first tower was sold out before it was even built, which is a good sign for a second tower.

10:30 A.M. I go downstairs to do the voiceovers for *The Apprentice.* It's great having the equipment on the premises, and it's become almost second nature to me.

11:00 A.M. Don Jr. and Ivanka, who are both on the development team, and Jason Greenblatt, executive vice president and general counsel, come in to go over some plans for the Dubai project, as well as the Panama Ocean Club. Things are going international lately.

11:45 A.M. Don Jr. stays and Jill Cremer, vice president of development, and Andy Weiss, executive vice president of construction, come in to discuss the health club in the Chicago tower that's going up. This building is on a wonderful site and will be a great addition to the great skyline of Chicago.

12:15 P.M. I return some calls and ask for some pizza and a diet Coke. It's rare that I go out for lunch. I keep this tradition because going out for lunch interrupts the day, so I keep it to a minimum. I go over some mail and documents.

12:45 P.M. Allen Weisselberg, my chief financial officer, comes in to go over some things, and we ask Jeff McConney and Eric Sacher, my controllers, to come in, too. This team has been with me a long time.

1:30 P.M. I record a 20th anniversary sound bite for Rosanna Scotto, followed by a meeting with Cathy Glosser, vice president of licensing, about the upcoming Eyewear Trade Show at the Javits Center.

2:00 P.M. I take a call from the *San Francisco Chronicle* about my March 26 speech in San Francisco. Then I call Bill Zanker—a very energetic guy and a great promoter—who runs the Learning Annex events. He tells me they are expecting 61,000 people at the Moscone Center in San Francisco—could be one of the biggest crowds yet. We had a great speech event in Dallas recently, so I'm inclined to believe what Bill is predicting.

2:30 P.M. I call Mark Burnett. *The Apprentice* will be shooting in Los Angeles for the next season, starting in June, which will be an exciting change. We will be having a casting call here at Trump Tower later in the month for season six, and we had one in Los Angeles earlier in the month. While there, I appeared on the *Ellen DeGeneres Show* and on *Larry King.* I enjoy the time I spend in Los Angeles, which is good since I'll be spending more time there this year.

I ask Keith Schiller, my security chief, to come in to discuss the plans for Los Angeles. We talk about our last trip there, which included a visit to my golf course in Palos Verdes, Trump National Golf Club Los Angeles. I played at Pebble Beach earlier this year and we agreed that the two courses are at least equal to each other in beauty. California is lucky to have two of the great golf courses in the world.

3:00 P.M. George Steinbrenner calls—always a great call to receive. There's no one like George. We talk about opening day at Yankee Stadium, which is on April 11. I'll definitely be there.

It won't be announced until April, but I am planning to donate 436 acres in New York City's northern suburbs for a new state park. It's estimated to be worth $100 million, but I think New Yorkers deserve it.

3:30 P.M.   Rhona comes in with a pile of mail that is at least a foot high and some other things for me to look through. I ask her to hold my calls while I give it a shot. Lots of mail comes with the territory. I should be used to it, but sometimes it can seem endless.

4:30 P.M.   I start returning calls, including calls back to Howard Lorber and Ashley Cooper. Ashley runs my golf course in New Jersey, and we talk about Tartan Day to be held at Trump National Golf Club Bedminster. My golf clubs have done extremely well, and they are fantastic to play. Being a golfer makes a big difference when you are a golf course developer. I always ask myself, "Would I want to play here?" Because I have high standards, you can bet the courses will be the best.

5:30 P.M.   Matthew Calamari, the chief operating officer of Trump Properties, comes in to discuss various things. Matthew's been with me for close to 25 years, and it looks like things are under control. I ask him what he thinks of some chairs I've been looking at for one of my golf clubs and we decide to go downstairs to see the new lobby showcases.

6:30 P.M.   I decide to head home. It's been a long day, so I take the elevator up to my apartment.

5

WITHOUT KNOWLEDGE, YOU DON'T STAND A CHANCE

*Gain and use information
to your advantage*

Obtain knowledge and learn everything you can about each project you undertake. If you enter a deal without sufficient knowledge, you will be throwing away your time and money. It's like playing high-stakes poker without knowing the rules—you're bound to lose because there are plenty of sharks who can't wait to take a sucker's money.

Study your area of business. All business involves risk, but risk can be greatly reduced when you learn everything you can about what you're doing. Gain knowledge so that you can make better decisions and become the best. Everyone wants to deal with the best, but no one wants to deal with a dummy—except to take his money.

A funny thing about knowledge is that once you start obtaining it, it becomes addictive. As you become better informed, your understanding improves, you become more of an expert, and your interest turns into a passion. People recognize your knowledge and respect you for it. They come to you for advice, which is flattering and helpful because they're usually glad to help you in return.

When you acquire knowledge, it makes you a more interesting and interested person. Start early and keep learning regardless of your age or accomplishments. If you continue to learn, you will develop a cutting-edge mentality that will help you succeed and develop new interests.

In college, I spent my spare time reading about real estate and foreclosures. I read on my own because I was interested and truly wanted to learn, not just to pass a test. My extracurricular studying led to my first successful real estate deal in which I earned enough money to start building my own business. I found a 1,200-unit residential development that had 800 vacant apartments. It was a disaster. Although the developers had gone under and the government foreclosed, I saw it as a great opportunity. I worked hard and learned a lot, which gave me confidence and increased my thirst to move forward in my real estate career.

I've continued the pattern I began with that first deal throughout my life: Before I commit to any venture, I study it fully because I want to know all the facts.

RESEARCH PAYS OFF

When I was interested in buying 40 Wall Street (the home of Trump University), I learned everything I could about the building and the current owner's troubles. I studied the building, the neighborhood, the market conditions, and anything remotely related. When the opportunity finally came to buy the building,

40 Wall Street.
Photo courtesy of the Trump Organization.

I was ready, and I knew exactly what I was getting. The tallest building in lower Manhattan, 40 Wall Street is a 1.3 million-square-foot landmark, and I bought it for $1.3 million. You can imagine what it's worth now, considering that it's hard to find a one-bedroom apartment in Manhattan for under $1 million these days.

INSIST ON PERFECTION

When I develop my golf courses, I call on the world's top experts. I literally ask hundreds of questions about every detail, tree, hole, and idea because I don't want to leave anything to chance. I want to identify the best products, people, and way to proceed. Fortunately, these experts love their work, so they don't find my questioning tedious. By the time construction begins, I know everything that needs to be done and how the entire project should proceed, which helps me stay informed as the project progresses.

The 10th Hole at The Trump National Golf Club in Los Angeles.
Photo courtesy of the Trump Organization.

Ignorance is inexcusable; it's the surest way to fail. No acceptable reason exists for not being well informed. Projects succeed when you create teams of experts who put their knowledge together and aim for the best. I take this approach and, because of it, my projects are spectacular.

The seeds of learning can grow almost anywhere, and you can never know too much about what you're doing.

—Donald J. Trump

Being well informed is a continuous and daily process. Our world now moves so quickly that keeping up is a challenge. Not keeping up is like quitting. Don't quit. Learn everything you can because you never know when it will come in handy.

I created Trump University because I want to impart the business knowledge that I've accumulated over the years. It's my way of stressing how important I feel it is to obtain knowledge. At Trump University, you get information in a practical, convenient setting that teaches success.

 MAKE IT HAPPEN IN YOUR LIFE

Here are some steps to help you gain more knowledge:

- Read constantly to learn everything you can about your interests from books, articles, and web sites.

- Make files to save important information you read. File the names of authors and business movers and shakers. Visit their web sites to learn about their accomplishments.

- Contact successful businesspeople, authors, experts, and insiders and try to meet them or ask for their advice. Use your network contacts to help you. Find out if these experts regularly attend conferences, conventions, or other events.

Ask Mr. Trump: Questions from Readers of the Trump University Blog

Q: I'm in a full-time MBA program at one of the top business schools. What can I do to get the best return on my investment of time and money?

DJT: Go beyond what your classes require and study on your own. Find an area that interests you and then learn all you can about it. Better yet, get involved in the area to gain experience. No matter where you go to school, you can always supplement what you learn in your courses with your own studies. Then your time and investment will be put to good use.

6

YOU'RE FIRED!

Words no one wants to hear—or say

Despite all I've accomplished, all the projects I've developed, and the amazing organization I've built, it's ironic that I'm most known for the phrase, "You're fired!" It shows the power of television. Total strangers walk up, point their fingers at me, cock them sharply, and say, "You're fired!" Then they laugh like crazy and announce to their companions, "I just fired the Donald."

I'm delighted to give them a good laugh and to know that they watch *The Apprentice*. I've also come to terms with being so closely identified with a phrase that no one likes to hear or say.

Firing anyone, even the worst, most unpleasant, inept jerk, isn't fun. It can also be very disruptive to your business. Making the decision to fire an employee can be agonizing, and actually firing the worker can be tough to carry out.

Fired workers can become hostile, as can their friends who may still work for you.

Firing an employee can leave your business in a hole; that's why so many companies hang on to less-than-desirable workers. To replace an employee, you have to go through the entire costly and time-consuming hiring process again. But frequently, you have no choice. If your business is to move forward, unproductive people must go.

Businesses are complex organizations that depend on many people to perform. When a link in the chain malfunctions or doesn't satisfactorily perform, the entire organization suffers and goals may not be met, so you may have to eliminate the weak link.

Firing can be an essential and a responsible business decision. It isn't pleasant, but lopping off a branch can save the tree.

—Donald J. Trump

PLAY BY THE BOOK

Firing workers involves a major risk, so don't do it without appropriate consideration. Fired employees often become disgruntled and sue their ex-employers—some have received outrageously high damage awards.

Protect yourself by developing rules that govern why and how you may fire employees and then follow these rules to the letter. Consult an employment law attorney and have him or her write or review your firing rules and procedures. Think of it as an investment that will be well worth the cost. Just one lawsuit, even if you win, can disrupt your business and cost a fortune to defend. If you lose, it can put you out of business.

BEWARE

Never fire an employee when you're angry or when other workers are present. Don't let an employee bait you into losing your temper. If you feel yourself getting angry, immediately walk away. Go somewhere and cool down. When you are completely composed, discuss the situation with someone who can give you objective advice. Develop a plan on how to proceed and consider reviewing it with an attorney.

Don't blow up in front of your employees. When you're displeased with a worker, discuss your feelings with him or her privately, not in an open, public area or where other employees might watch and overhear. If you're concerned about meeting with an employee alone because he or she might become hostile, have another member of your staff sit in. Meet in a neutral place, not in your office, so you can get up and leave.

At termination meetings with employees, don't get drawn into arguments or debates. Be civil, polite, and businesslike. Expect the employee to be upset, so be direct and courteous, but give the employee a full opportunity to speak.

Fortunately, I seem to attract people who like to work hard and who get a sense of achievement from their efforts. Most of the people I've fired knew they weren't performing to a satisfactory level, and I've had very few problems in that area. I'm demanding but fair and they know it. There's a level of objectivity involved on both sides, which can be very helpful in these kinds of situations.

 Make It Happen in Your Life

Here are some tips on firing employees:

- Don't ignore employee performance problems. The sooner you talk with the employee, the more likely you can get him or her back on track. Getting great work from employees is a sign of a strong leader.

- See if an underperforming employee could improve with additional training, equipment, or switching tasks.

- If you believe improvement is possible, meet with the employee and give him or her a fixed period to deliver measurable results. Be clear about your requirements and state exactly what you expect, and specify that if what you need is not satisfactorily provided, he or she will be fired. Then follow through.

- Since firings can be emotional, it often helps to discuss the situation with an objective advisor before you actually dismiss an employee. It may be wise to speak with someone outside your organization who will have enough distance to give you sound advice. However, if you are convinced that someone in your organization will be objective, call on him or her.

- Think of people you could call to give you good advice, individuals who you respect. Which of them has the best judgment, understands the realities involved in running a business, and would be happy to help you? Come up with several names so if your first choice is not available, you can immediately call others on your list.

Ask Mr. Trump: Questions from Readers of the Trump University Blog

Q: Why are companies today so quick to lay off thousands of people, force salary cuts, lowball wages, and downscale benefits?

DJT: Most businesses watch the bottom line, and sometimes actions that seem drastic or unfair are necessary to remain in business. In the business world, no business means no jobs, but some business means some jobs. Always watch out for your best interests. If you think you're with an unfair or unscrupulous organization, look elsewhere. Try putting yourself in your employer's shoes; maybe he or she is trying to save the business and jobs. Then again, maybe he or she is not. Be fair in your assessment by trying to see it from both sides.

7

The Proof Is in the Doing

Learn by doing and taking risks

Some people are book smart but are clueless when dealing with the real world. Others are street smart but can't handle anything other than what they're used to. We based a season of *The Apprentice* on pitting highly educated candidates against those who had less formal schooling. When we examined how both teams performed, we found that the key to success was experience, not education. Experience comes from action, or *doing*, and entails taking risks. Knowledge is essential, but knowledge alone isn't enough. You must act on your knowledge—put it to work—because *doing* is how you learn and ultimately prove yourself.

Lord knows I've taken lots of risks and not all of them were rousing successes. Few things worth doing are risk free, so prepare to take risks. Don't always play it safe, but do try to minimize the dangers and know exactly how much you could lose. Frequently, the risk will be well worth the gamble, but sometimes it will be more than you can afford.

Most things take on new dimensions when you actually do them. Golf can seem easy and effortless until you try it. Suddenly, you see how hard it can be.

Don't underestimate anything until you try it. The pros make difficult maneuvers look easy because they've spent thousands of hours perfecting them. You probably haven't seen them practicing, but they constantly work to hone their craft and improve their art. Then, they go out and perform.

INSIST ON PERFECTION

When I was interested in acquiring the Commodore Hotel near Grand Central Station, a friend told the press that my idea was like "fighting for a seat on the Titanic." On paper, the odds were stacked against me, and the project seemed to be an enormous risk. But I had a vision and a plan that I knew would work.

So I jumped into the fray and put a complex project together. I built the Grand Hyatt Hotel, which not only became a huge success but also sparked redevelopment of the dilapidated area around Grand Central Station.

On that project, I learned by doing. I must admit that all the doubters who complained about how crummy the area had become motivated me to change it. My response was, "I'm going to do it and make it work instead of just finding fault."

You need hands-on involvement to understand a business and the problems you will face. You have to gain experience, and that only comes from actually doing—and doing often.

FEAR OF FAILURE

Many people are afraid to fail, so they don't try. They may dream, talk, and even plan, but they don't take that critical step of putting their money and their effort on the line. To succeed in business, you must take risks. Even if you fail, that's how you learn. There has never been, and will never be, an Olympic ice skater who didn't fall on the ice. Skaters acquire their skill and master their moves by doing and falling, not just by watching or talking.

Knowledge requires patience; action requires courage. Put patience and courage together and you'll be a winner.

—Donald J. Trump

 MAKE IT HAPPEN IN YOUR LIFE

Find challenges for yourself. Go beyond the ordinary.

- Look for opportunities that have some risk or situations that have kept others away. Find out why others held off and see if their fear is still valid. Everything changes, so deals people wouldn't touch before may now be viable

because of new developments, changed conditions, or
your unique talents.

- In your planning, know how much risk you can take.
  Evaluate whether the returns will be worth the risk, and
  set a firm limit on how much you can gamble.

- Examine ways to cut your risk. Sometimes it may be only
  tackling certain parts of a project or bringing in partners
  or associates to limit your risks.

Ask Mr. Trump: Questions from Readers of the Trump University Blog

Q: I'm finishing a course to help me pass my real estate sales
exam. Then, I'll need to keep my full-time job until my income
from selling real estate can support me full-time. Should I start in
residential sales part-time until I can switch to commercial full-
time or go straight to commercial real estate and try to find a firm
that will hire me part-time?

DJT: Take the risk. Go directly into commercial real estate. Based
on the skills, contacts, and effort required, you would be more
likely to succeed in commercial real estate if you did it full-time.
Gain a reputation for being a commercial real estate expert, not a
residential salesperson who dabbles in other things. If I'm looking
for somebody to lease my office building, I want somebody who
will work on it full-time. If I were looking for somebody to sell my
commercial building, I would look for someone who has expertise in that area.

Commercial real estate is a tougher business to break into.
Almost anybody can be a residential broker, but it's hard to land
your first commercial real estate deal because people want to deal
with someone with experience. Some commercial real estate
firms may give you draws or let you do other work assisting bro-
kers, which would give you income while you learn and gain
experience.

8

YOUR GUT IS YOUR
BEST ADVISOR

Listen to your instincts

Within seconds of meeting Mark Burnett, the creator of *The Apprentice*, I knew he was 100 percent solid, both as a person and as a professional. Right away, I liked and trusted Mark, and I knew that I wanted to do business with him. However, I've met people who I've had an immediate aversion to even though I never knew why. While I try not to be judgmental, I've learned to listen to and trust my gut. It's one of my most valued counselors.

Most of us have sharply honed instincts—deeply imbedded likes, dislikes, and feelings—that are as much a part of us as our limbs. Ignoring these instincts is like not trusting your eyes, but we frequently do ignore them—usually to our regret. It's easy to

Donald J. Trump with Allen Weisselberg, EVP, CFO, Trump Organization.
Photo courtesy of the Trump Organization.

question our feelings, especially when they're contrary to what other people believe. We may think that we are being illogical, overly emotional, or unreasonable, so we disregard how we feel. Usually, that's a big mistake!

I trust my instincts because they are the product of everything that went into making me who I am. They reflect the essential me—my values, feelings, fears, experiences, and goals. Instincts are the distillation of the lessons we learned from our parents, families, teachers, and friends. They're based on all our experiences in life, especially when we got burned. Our instincts are the logic we've developed from living, doing, watching, listening. They guide us, protect us, and remind us who we really are.

Problems arise when our instincts don't seem logical or con-sistent with the facts, and we don't know which to trust. I try to get all the information, examine all the facts, and then I usually follow my gut.

Follow your instincts. You alone know where you really want to go.

—Donald J. Trump

USE YOUR INSTINCTS

It takes strength to follow your instincts when everyone and everything insists you're wrong. It's hard to stand alone, against the tide of differing opinion and all the solid evidence produced by high-priced and acclaimed experts. Sometimes that's just what you must do. You have to listen to your inner voices and trust what they tell you to do.

In the final analysis, the responsibility for making decisions lies with you. It's your life, family, business, money, or choice.

When I first started building golf courses, my instincts told me it was a good business decision. I knew if I combined my pas-sion for golf with my knowledge of the process, I would succeed. I found the best golf course designers in the world and spent many hours working with them. The results have been spectacu-lar because I merged instinct and logic with the confidence that I would succeed.

I was once asked, if I were in a jungle, would I prefer to have a guide or a map. I'd choose a guide. If you correctly interpret your feelings and instincts, they will be the valuable guide that gives you an edge.

COACH TRUMP · MAKE IT HAPPEN IN YOUR LIFE

Going with your gut can keep you intact. Remember that being whole reinforces your strength.

- Identify your values and most cherished beliefs. Reinforce in your mind what is most important to you. Simply thinking about your values will influence the decisions you make.

- Trust your feelings, but also listen to reason. Stay open to new ways and ideas so that you and your instincts will continue to grow.

BEWARE

Some people use the excuses, "That's how I feel"; "That's who I am"; and "This is how it always worked for me, and I'm not going to change." These people are really just afraid of change.

Change is good and necessary. On occasion, it can be good to go against your instincts and habits just to shake things up, to see life from another perspective, or simply to take a chance. Repetition can put you to sleep. Sometimes you have to look for opportunities to respond differently and break the mold.

Ask Mr. Trump: Questions from Readers of the Trump University Blog

Q: How do you develop your instincts and distinguish intuition from fear or doubt?

DJT: It takes practice. Sometimes the answers are very clear, and you'll just know. Other times you'll feel indecisive for good reason. Often it means the timing is not right. That's when hesitating is good. I've been very glad that I waited on certain matters because the extra time helped me get ready and make the opportunity right.

We all get indications in different ways, so learn to read your clues. Arrange to take some quiet time for yourself every day because it's hard to think clearly when you're always surrounded by commotion. Sometimes, we have to tune out to tune in.

A Very Special Week (Plus) in My Life . . .

Tuesday

8:30 A.M. Paula Shugart, president of Miss Universe, arrives for a meeting about the new *Miss Universe Guide to Beauty* book launch that will be held in Trump Tower in April. We also discuss the Miss Universe Pageant to be held in Los Angeles, California, in July and the Miss USA Pageant that will be in Baltimore, Maryland, in April. The pageants have done extremely well, and the book should be a winner, too. Paula has done a terrific job.

9:30 A.M. Andy Weiss comes in to talk about the Chicago buyout for roofing.

I ask Andi Rowntree, an executive assistant, if she would be interested in staying in Los Angeles for the next season's *Apprentice* shoots in Los Angeles. She thinks it will be a good experience and she agrees to stay there for a couple of months.

10:00 A.M. I have a meeting with Michael Sexton, president of Trump University, to go over some details. I've always been interested in education and making it accessible is a great way to go. I ask Meredith McIver to join us to go over the schedule of essays we're preparing for a book.

10:45 A.M. Regis Philbin calls to remind me that he thinks Regis would be a great name if we have a baby boy. Regis can always be counted on for great ideas.

11:00 A.M. I call Terry Lundgren about the upcoming weekend because he'll be one of my guests at Mar-a-Lago.

Don Jr. and Ivanka come in with some possible changes to the design of the tower in Dubai.

My kids stay on top of things and have given me reason to trust their opinions and instincts about the business. By the way, my son Eric will be graduating from Georgetown in May. All my kids are hard workers, and I'm very proud of them.

11:30 A.M. I call Melania to see how she's doing. Even with a baby due soon, she keeps a busy schedule and is still as beautiful as ever. She will be a wonderful mother.

11:45 A.M. Kim Mogull comes in for a meeting about Megu, a restaurant to open in Trump World Tower in April. This will be a fantastic location for an equally fantastic restaurant.

12:30 P.M. I call the Trump Grill in Trump Tower and ask Chris Devine, the executive chef, for something good to eat. He knows I'm trying to be healthy, but since we're not far from St. Patrick's Day, he sends up some corned beef and cabbage, which tastes great.

12:45 P.M. I take a call from Robert Kiyosaki, author of *Rich Dad Poor Dad,* which has once again become the number one best seller on the *New York Times* list. We are working on a book together, so he's visited my offices a few times, plus we see each other regularly at Learning Annex events. Robert and his beautiful wife Kim are very successful people, and they are also very happy people.

I call Sharon Lechter, Robert Kiyosaki's partner and coauthor, to see how the folks are doing over at Time Warner because she deals with them on occasion. Time Warner published *TrumpNation,* a ridiculous book full of untruths, so I decided to sue for $5 billion.

1:30 P.M. I have a meeting with Sonia Talesnik, assistant general counsel, about some events at Trump World Tower and the upcoming meeting with the new Trump World Tower board members.

2:00 P.M.   Paula White, also known as Pastor Paula, stops by
for a visit. Paula has had incredible success and she
remains as genuine as ever.

I talk to Rana Williams, a broker who has been
with me for years, and then to Susan James, the
on-site broker for Trump International Hotel & Tower
since it opened. Both of these women have done a
tremendous job and dealing with them is always
enjoyable. I think their clients are lucky people.

2:30 P.M.   Norma Foerderer calls to tell me that she's read Abe
Wallace's book manuscript called *Ten Years Working
with Donald Trump* and that it's well done. It
includes stories of some of the great projects that we
worked on, and I look forward to reading it.

My makeup artist Sharon Sinclair arrives for
The Apprentice shoot. Sharon has been with me for
a few years now, and it's always nice to see her. I
decide I should go upstairs and change my shirt for
today's shoot.

4:00 P.M.   The crowds were pretty big downstairs, but everyone
was well behaved so the shoot went well. It's one of
those perfect spring days today so there's a lot of foot
traffic on Fifth Avenue. It's hard to imagine that three
years ago *The Apprentice* was just an idea, not a reality.
Many things have changed since then—one being
the crowds that appear. It makes me realize the power
of the media. I was famous before, but not like this.

I have read some of the mail for today. One letter
was from my kindergarten teacher, a kind woman
named Hildegard Stoeltzing. She mentioned that she
remembers me because I never stopped asking
questions. I decided to write her back, telling her
that some things never change. I still ask questions,
but it has served me well. I also wanted to thank her,
belatedly, for her patience.

There was a letter from the mother of a young man
named Jared who is enduring chemotherapy. She
told me how her son told her not to be sad because
he knew that people often have a down before they

have an up. She asked him where he learned that, and he said "Donald Trump. He has been down several times, and he always comes back up. Mr. Trump is back up now, and he helps many people do the same thing." That made me feel great, so I decided to send the young man some gifts and a note with a hope that he will get better soon.

4:30 P.M. I call Melania to see what she'd like to do for dinner. We decide we'll order in.

I take a call from Jim Dowd, who now has his own agency, about some upcoming events, including a Hair Cuttery recording, because Jim's agency promotes *The Apprentice.*

Don Jr. comes in to go over some details with me. We both tend to be meticulous about details, which is a good thing considering the business we're in.

5:15 P.M. Nathan Nelson, vice president, comes in to go over some insurance issues. Nathan is thorough, which is always appreciated.

I have a meeting with Michelle Lokey, staff attorney, to discuss some contracts. Michelle appeared on *The Apprentice* a couple of seasons ago and has done a great job.

5:45 P.M. Andy Litinsky, project manager, stops by to give me an update. You might remember Andy from *The Apprentice II*—he was the youngest candidate and the debate champ from Harvard. On the show, he was fired, but in reality, I hired him. I knew he'd be a good fit for the Trump Organization, and I was right.

6:00 P.M. Rhona comes in to go over some speech dates and contracts. At 6:30, I take the rest of the mail and go home.

9

PERSONALIZE YOUR PITCH

Know who you're addressing

Know who you're talking to and where he or she is coming from. Whether you're involved in negotiations, war, public speaking, or merely socializing, learn about the person across from you and find out what he or she wants so that you can build a better relationship.

Frequently, people are so involved in trying to get what they want that they don't think of anyone other than themselves. They're so overcome with the brilliance of their idea that they ignore other people's needs and objectives and don't successfully connect.

At every level, relationships are built on listening, connections, common interests, and experiences. It is essential to be able to read your audience, whether that audience consists of a couple of people in your office or 40,000 in an amphitheater listening to you speak. The challenge is to find common ground.

Speaking at the Learning Annex Wealth Expo.
Photo courtesy of the Trump Organization.

I was involved in a very difficult negotiation and found myself disliking my adversary. My feelings placed a wall between us; my dislike made our dealings strained and unproductive. Our deal was on the verge of collapsing, when I discovered that my adversary was an avid golfer like myself. When we began our next session, I mentioned that I had heard he was a golfer. We started talking about golf, which eased the tension. When we resumed our business, we were more at ease, communicated more easily, and closed the deal.

I've heard stories about people who landed terrific jobs, not just because of their qualifications, but also because of common interests they had with the people hiring them. Granted, the applicant had to have the credentials to begin with, but lots of people do. A top law firm hired a young lawyer because, in addition to excelling in law school, he held a master's degree in music. His music degree was the deciding factor because the partner who interviewed him also happened to be a musicologist and knew how much discipline it took to earn a music degree. The fact that they both were devoted to music provided them with a common bond that could help them work better together.

GET THE AUDIENCE'S ATTENTION

Comedians and top public speakers are experts at sizing up an audience and personalizing their pitch. Comedians usually start by saying something that relates specifically to the group they are performing for. They immediately capture the audience's attention and create a bond; audiences think of the comedian as a member of the group. At that point, the audience likes the comedian, is attentive, and buys into what he or she says.

Determine what you have in common with anyone you deal with and lead with it. If you take the time, you can create a bond that didn't previously exist. For example, if you get stuck in traffic on the way to an event, chances are others will have had this experience also. Most everyone from billionaires to struggling single moms or students have been forced to sit idly in traffic jams. If you open with a comment about the awful traffic, you may see a room full of people vigorously nodding their heads in agreement.

Smart businesspeople prepare for every situation; they do their homework by analyzing the market, knowing who their buyers are, and personalizing their pitch. That's the way to the top.

After I spoke to an audience of more than 40,000 people, a member of my staff asked me if addressing such a large group made me nervous. I answered no because I went on stage knowing who I would be addressing and I was fully prepared to interest them. I had investigated who would be in the audience, what they had in common, why they would be attending, and what they wanted to learn. Then, I tried to give them what they wanted in a way they could identify with.

When you're prepared, there's no reason to be nervous. Treat any speech or any pitch as an opportunity to shine— and you usually will. Always deliver the goods by giving your audience valuable information, no matter how many people are in the room.

—Donald J. Trump

 MAKE IT HAPPEN IN YOUR LIFE

There is usually a common bond with your audience. Your job is to find it.

- Before you deal with others, find out all you can about them. Learn about their backgrounds, interests, and ambitions, and look for anything you have in common.

- When you come across common denominators, figure out the best way to raise them. I find it's best to be direct: "Hey, I heard that you play golf." If the other person doesn't respond positively, don't force the issue.

- Don't overlook any opportunity to break the ice. Every- day occurrences such the weather or current events can be good starting points. They affect all of us, whether we're billionaires or college students, and can ease us into better communications.

- At the end of the meeting or in a confirming or follow-up e-mail, briefly mention or refer to the item you have in common. These asides add a touch of personal warmth that can strengthen your relationship.

Ask Mr. Trump: Questions from Readers of the Trump University Blog

Q: I'm starting a small business, and I have a clear vision of what I want my business to become. What do you think are the five most important aspects to consider when opening a small business in a small but global (when tourism is considered) town?

DJT:

1. Know the market.

2. Do your research.

3. Go with your gut. Trust your instincts.

4. Be prepared to work every single day at full capacity.

5. Don't give up—ever. Be tough and tenacious.

10

SURROUND YOURSELF
WITH BEAUTY

Enhance every aspect of your life

Everyone knows how important beauty is to me. I always try to have it in my life. I hire the best people, find the most fabulous locations, and use the finest materials to make sure that every project I undertake is truly exceptional. Being surrounded by beauty makes me feel great; it enhances every part of my life, and I deserve it.

Beauty and elegance, whether in a woman, a building, or a work of art, is not just superficial or something pretty to see. Beauty and elegance are products of personal style that come from deep within. No matter how hard you try, you cannot buy style. It has an intrinsic value, and for me, style and success are completely interwoven. I wouldn't want to have one without the other.

Sky View of Mar-a-Lago.
Photo courtesy of the Trump Organization.

My style is based on trying to make whatever I do breathtakingly beautiful. People react emotionally to my style; they appreciate, get pleasure from, and want more of it. My style excites me and inspires me to do bigger, better, and more magnificent projects. It's no accident that I'm so involved with beauty; it's my signature, my brand, and I think it's best to have it in spades.

Think about what you find to be beautiful: What really knocks you out? Bring it into your life; get involved. If it's people, get to know and spend quality time with them; build strong relationships with them. If your interest is places, experiences, or ideas, find ways to visit, participate in, or explore them. When you are drawn to material objects, consider acquiring them if you can.

When successful people surround themselves with beauty, it's generally assumed that they are indulging themselves, buying themselves trophies, or showing off. Although some of that may be true, contact with beauty provides much more. It exposes successful people to an excellence from which they can learn, grow, and improve their lives. Beauty rewards people for all their hard work.

When you're exposed to beauty, you will want to bring elements of it into other parts of your life. That can help you rise to higher levels. It can elevate your understanding of excellence and the quality of the goods or services you provide. Instead of just delivering good, serviceable items, this new understanding can drive you to furnish only the very best.

Beauty is normally an asset, not a liability. A beautiful woman on *The Apprentice* complained that her beauty was a liability, but I felt that her attitude was the actual liability.

—Donald J. Trump

When you're planning your projects, it's not that much more difficult or expensive to make them beautiful. If what you provide is exceptional, you can increase your price. Beauty will also enhance your reputation because it tells the world that you have excellent standards and consistently produce the most beautiful work. People will want to be associated with you and your projects because it implies that they also have great taste.

When you have beauty in your life, it can make everything better and more worthwhile. Isn't that the reason you work so hard?

 MAKE IT HAPPEN IN YOUR LIFE

If you keep in touch with your goals by visualizing them, they stand a good chance of working out beautifully.

- Identify what really excites you. What do you find beautiful? Some objects may not be readily obtainable, or you may have to wait for years to purchase them, but don't give up; it will give you a goal to shoot for.

- List the most direct ways that you can bring beauty into your life. Can you simply go out and buy it? Can you make it or have it made for you? Can you approach it yourself? Do you need others to introduce you to it or help you get it?

- If you need the help of others, list who they are and how you can reach them. Before contacting them, decide what you will ask them. If you need additional knowledge, training, or qualifications, identify exactly what that would be.

- Create a step-by-step plan of attack and systematically implement it. Make a backup plan that you can use if your first efforts don't work.

11

NEGOTIATE TO WIN

Use diplomacy

I've been called a master negotiator because I usually get what I want. I negotiate to win, and then I win. My process, however, isn't necessarily what you would expect. I spend lots of time preparing for negotiations, which usually gives me the edge.

When most people hear the word negotiation, they usually picture stone-faced adversaries who glare at each other across a conference table and argue over every little point. That's not how I work. A better example is how I went about buying 40 Wall Street.

I was interested in acquiring 40 Wall Street for years. I followed the building as the neighborhood changed, tenants moved out, and real estate values plunged. I watched as it changed hands and was finally purchased by the Hinneberg family who ran it from Germany. I learned as much as I could about the family, including how they conducted business and the problems they were having with the property.

When I decided to make my move, I knew that the family's agent handled all the business for the building. Although everyone dealt with the agent, I wanted to meet with the Hinnebergs face to face to find out what they wanted and to explain my vision. If you want to learn the truth, try to bypass the agents and handlers and go to the owner.

So I flew to Germany and met the Hinnebergs. They were impressed that I devoted so much time and effort to meet them. It showed the depth of my commitment. The Hinnebergs reacted favorably when I assured them that I would turn the property into a first-class office building, which I have. We didn't sit down at a table and fight. Instead, we put our cards on the table and talked. We soon came to terms. All my preparation paid off, and we struck a deal in which we all won.

PERSUASION

I believe that the key to striking a deal is persuasion, not power. Persuasion is diplomacy at its best—the ability to convince people to accept your ideas. You don't want to force people to accept your ideas. That's a recipe for disaster. Instead, you want them to think that the decision was theirs, which gives them a greater sense of power and control. Your objective should be to make your adversaries feel like they're your partners, not your victims. Present your ideas in a way that will not intimidate your adversaries or make them feel that they are being forced to surrender. In successful negotiations, all parties should feel satisfied with the outcome.

Donald J. Trump with Mark Burnett of Mark Burnett Productions.
Photo courtesy of The Mark Burnett Productions.

Don't let your expectations confine you. Sometimes you have to switch gears, change your plans, play psychologist, or be a bit of a chameleon to figure out the best negotiating approach.

—Donald J. Trump

I wanted to deal with a member of a prominent family, and although I knew his name, we had never met. Even so, I had developed assumptions about him. Before our meeting, I created a plan, but when I met the guy, his insecurity and unassuming demeanor surprised me. He was not the powerhouse I imagined, so I immediately changed my plan. I realized that if we went to battle, he would probably walk away to avoid the confrontation. I had to boost his esteem to get him to negotiate, so I gently worked to build his trust and confidence. My approach worked, and we did business.

 MAKE IT HAPPEN IN YOUR LIFE

Negotiation is about preparation. It's not a mysterious process, but it can be exhilarating. See it as an art and be meticulous.

- Prepare thoroughly for any negotiation by defining your objectives. Know the minimum you must receive to make the deal and the maximum you will pay. If you can't strike a deal within that framework, be ready to walk away.

- Know what the other side wants. Learn your adversary's strengths and weaknesses: Find out who your adversaries are, what resources they have, who is backing them, how much they want, why they want it, how much they will settle for, and how much they will pay or insist on receiving.

- Stick to the facts; don't guess, generalize, or listen to what others believe. Get proof, documentation, and solid figures. No two people, companies, ventures, or proposals are the same, so don't assume or jump to conclusions. Verify, check, and examine—find out for yourself.

- When you negotiate, be fair and reasonable so everyone can win. Don't demand everything and risk making an enemy who could come back to haunt you.

Ask Mr. Trump: Questions from Readers of the Trump University Blog

Q: I'm in a family business. My family is satisfied with keeping the company where it is, but I want to take it to the next level. What can I do?

DJT: Show your family a solid plan that lays out your proposal. Then convince them that it's a good idea. This may call for some negotiation skill. The best negotiations occur when everyone wins. Explain to your family how everyone will benefit from your plan and be thorough. Don't generalize or be vague; give them facts, figures, and numbers. Remember the golden rule of negotiating: He who has the gold makes the rules.

12

THINK ON YOUR FEET

It's the fast track to success

When I started in business, I spent a lot of my time researching every detail that could affect the deals I was considering. I still do today. People often comment on how quickly I think on my feet, and they think I've had this gift from birth. Actually, I make decisions quickly because I always do my homework. I prepare by examining everything that might be involved in a deal. Outsiders never see the thorough research, detailed preparation, analysis, and all the other preliminary work. They see only the results, which are just the tip of the iceberg. Like a well-trained athlete, I prepare thoroughly, and then when the time is right, I'm ready to spring from the gate. Ironically, learning to be spontaneous takes preparation and practice.

The Apprentice teaches candidates to think quickly on their feet. Since they're placed under tight time constraints, they have to think, act, and express themselves without hesitation or they lose and are fired by me. Since their ideas don't always work, they also need backup plans that they can employ when Plan A fails. If they're ready and move promptly and decisively on Plan B, they can recover without losing much time. Learning to think ahead, be prepared, and to cover all the bases is essential to success.

Being able to think on your feet and get your point across clearly is crucial at every level of business, from an initial interview to a high-level board of directors meeting. In business, everyone needs quick, accurate answers and information. If you can't provide those answers, people won't forget. The effectiveness of your communication will be a major factor in determining whether you succeed and how high you rise. Invest in your future by mastering this essential art.

BE PREPARED

Few people are naturally gifted extemporaneous speakers, but most can learn. It usually takes training, experience, and discipline. If you want to learn how to talk on your feet, know your subject inside out so that you will never have to hesitate or bluff because questions will not surprise or stump you. You'll know every answer, and each question will give you a great opportunity to show how good you are and how much you know.

Master your subject; know it cold. Work at it, read about it, and discuss it with others. Dedicate yourself to working at it every day. Follow the example of great athletes who always train and push themselves to their limits. Accomplished athletes have great discipline and businesspeople should too.

A leader has the right to be beaten, but never the right to be surprised.

—Napoleon

Test your ability to respond by asking yourself random questions and then trying to answer them. The value of preparation cannot be overestimated, and if you want to be the best, you must excel at thinking on those feet of yours.

 MAKE IT HAPPEN IN YOUR LIFE

Henry Ford said, *"If you think you can or if you think you can't, you're right."* It's best to think you can, and do something about making it happen.

- Master your subject. Become an expert in your area of business. Learn and think about every aspect of your field so that you can immediately rattle off answers to any questions.

- Take acting or public speaking classes or get media training. Invest in yourself by getting training; it will help you in every aspect of your career and life.

- Practice, practice, practice.

A Very Special Week (Plus) in My Life . . .

Wednesday

8:30 A.M. I do a short charity video for a former *Apprentice* candidate in the small conference room.

9:00 A.M. George Ross comes into my office to cover some *Apprentice* issues and other things. George is as rock solid as he appears on the show.

9:30 A.M. Rhona reminds me that the *Sopranos* season premiere is at the Museum of Modern Art and that I will be doing *The View* this morning. Their studios are on the West Side, so I will do a property check of Trump International Hotel & Tower, which is also on the West Side, on the way back to the office. That hotel was voted the number one hotel in New York City, but I'm not one to rest on my laurels. I decide to give Tom Downing, the general manager, a call. He's done a great job.

10:00 A.M. I do a guest appearance on *The View.* Television appearances have become part of my day job now, but I enjoy the live audiences and have a good time with them.

11:00 A.M. I take a call from the *San Francisco Business Journal* about my upcoming speech in San Francisco.
I do a walk-through of the Asprey store, located in Trump Tower, with Michelle Lokey and Bernie Diamond. That's a beautiful space and location.

11:30 A.M. I go upstairs briefly to my apartment to check on Melania; she's doing fine. One of my great luxuries is taking an elevator to and from work.

12:00 P.M.	I call down to Mar-a-Lago to talk to Berndt Lembcke about the Fireman's Ball at Mar-a-Lago in April. I will be given an honorary fire chief award. That will be a memorable evening.

Mar-a-Lago

I take a press call from Scotland about my upcoming trip there and the golf course plans I have.

Joe Cinque, director of the American Academy of Hospitality Sciences, stops by for a few minutes to visit. Joe travels everywhere and always has insights into the latest places. He still says the Mar-a-Lago Club is the best in the world.

12:30 P.M.	I have some delicious meatloaf from the Trump Grill downstairs. It should be tasty—it's my mother's recipe.

I call my sister Maryanne to see what's new. She's a judge and we're all very proud of her.

I get the bad news—again—that the Trump Tower escalators, which we have already replaced completely, are on the blink again. That's maddening because it took months to replace them and to make sure they were perfect. Ever since, we've had nothing but problems with them. I'm determined to solve this mess. There's a great deal of traffic these days in Trump Tower, and we can't afford to have anything that doesn't run smoothly and efficiently.

1:00 P.M.	Don Jr., Ivanka, and the development team come in to give me an update. I have to admit that a great deal is going on, but it's exciting and everyone is enthusiastic and plugged in. It's a good feeling. I hope I've demonstrated to my children and employees the importance of being diligent about everyday things. Everyday work leads to great achievements in the long run, but you can't ever become complacent, no matter how successful you are.

I take a call from Tom Pienkos, vice president of operations, and from Vinnie Stellio, executive vice president of development, to get an overview on some projects. Vinnie's been traveling often between my properties in Los Angeles and New York and has some good updates for me.

2:00 P.M. I have a photo shoot for *Forbes* magazine—a great publication.

2:15 P.M. As I've said many times, if you don't have problems, then you don't have a job. I guess I have a job, because the copy machine is on the blink again. That's another maddening thing. We have men walking on the moon, yet we still have copy machines that will not work more than a few days without breaking. It's a great mystery to me.

2:30 P.M. I have a phone interview with *Crain's New York Business* magazine. Then, the *San Jose Mercury News* calls about my San Francisco appearance. I'm looking forward to speaking, but I have to wonder if I am ready for 61,000 people. I can remember when my father spoke to 30 people in a room and it seemed like a big deal. Things have definitely changed. I sometimes wonder what my father would think if he could see the size of the crowds that I address.

3:00 P.M. I have a meeting with Rhona and I begin to review a couple of books that have been sent with a request for a foreword or a jacket blurb. I'm never lacking in reading material, that's for sure.
After that, I go through some mail and take a few calls. I have always multitasked, even before I knew the word.

4:00 P.M. I talk to the Credit Suisse people because I will be speaking at a luncheon for their real estate conference in early April.
I have a *New York Post* photo shoot for Trump Mortgage—a new service I have started. I expect it to

be an effective company, and it makes sense. A lot of things I am doing now are things I thought of but had to postpone until the time was right.

Ivanka comes in to tell me she will be appearing on the *Tonight Show* in early April. She's accustomed to the media, which has helped tremendously in her job. She's naturally poised and articulate—a big plus.

5:00 P.M. I go over some interview requests with Rhona and while it's nice to be wanted, sometimes it can seem overwhelming. We discuss whether to get a new ice-making machine in the office, and it looks like we will. Ours has been producing icebergs lately.

I decide to walk down the hall and visit Allen Weisselberg and my accounting team. Looks like everyone is busy and we've doubled up in some of the office spaces. Mark Burnett's team moved out of the floor below us, so we can expand to another floor. It's starting to look like a dorm in some of the offices, so it's time.

6:00 P.M. Back in my office, I go over a pile of documents and articles and make notes to be distributed. Then I see the two-foot stack of magazines I have yet to review, so I decide to take a foot's worth with me and go upstairs.

13

WORK WITH PEOPLE YOU LIKE

It sure beats working with enemies

When new employees work out, I sometimes credit it to divine intervention because people who interview well don't always perform as well on the job. Either way, it helps if you like having them around. I've been fortunate to work with people I like. Some of my employees have been with me for 20, 25, even 30 years. If we didn't like each other, we would be serving a long sentence of misery. As it is, we work well together, respect each other, and get more accomplished. Management becomes much easier if you are careful when choosing your employees and partners.

INSIST ON PERFECTION

Whoever works for me has to move fast. That's how I work, and my employees must follow suit. Jason Greenblatt, executive vice president and general counsel, can explain the most complex matters in 10 words or less. Considering how much I have on my plate every day, I appreciate his brevity. Allen Weisselberg, my chief financial officer, can be equally succinct, as can Bernie Diamond, executive vice president and general counsel, and Matthew Calamari, my chief operating officer who has been here for 23 years. It's not that I don't enjoy talking with them about nonbusiness matters, but our agendas have to be attended to and, by now, we all know how to get it done, individually and as a team.

Donald J. Trump with Matthew Calamari, EVP, COO, Trump Properties.
Photo courtesy of the Trump Organization.

INCREASE DIVERSITY TO ENJOY YOUR TIME

Most organizations continually evolve; I know the Trump Organization has. Different types of people come and go. Overall, I think it's good to have a balance of personalities and characters instead of a bunch of clones who are all basically the same. Such diversity can bring new, stimulating, and creative ideas to the business.

In New York City, you have no choice; diversity comes with the terrain. You may end up working with people who are completely different than you, or who you don't understand. They may have different values, traits, and goals, but you have to get along. The best part is that you can usually learn from these people, if you just give them a chance, and the differences can enrich your life. When you work with others, look beyond the obvious and how they present themselves. People are not one-dimensional. Every individual has unique talents that may or may not be in the job description or listed on a resume.

Most of us put in lots of time at our jobs. We probably spend more waking hours at work than we do with our families, so it's essential to create a pleasant, congenial, and efficient atmosphere. The people who work with me know that while I may be tough, I'm fair. Although I set the tone, my door is always open, and they can be confident that when they have something to say, I'll listen.

Set the example, and you'll be a magnet for the right people. That's the best way to work with people you like.

—Donald J. Trump

Good leaders determine the teams they assemble. If you pick the best players and set the example, many good seasons should follow.

- Think of your business as a team and of every employee as a team member who has a particular role to play. Then define each of those roles.

- Assemble a core group around you; create a great team. Fill in the group with people who will excel in their roles, who understand the company's needs, and who you like.

- Realize that each new hire will be somewhat of a gamble. Solid gold credentials don't guarantee solid gold employees, but sometimes they do.

BEWARE

Working with friends and relatives can become a nightmare. The line between work and family or friendships can disappear quickly and bad feelings can flare. If you have to fire a friend or relative, it can get ugly or impossible.

Since two of my children work for me, it shows that I like to live on the edge, but I know they are well prepared. It usually is preferable to become friendly with people at work but confine those relationships to the workplace.

Ask Mr. Trump: Questions from Readers of the Trump University Blog

Q: How should you manage people you don't like?

DJT: First find something you like about them. Everyone has hidden potential, and a good manager will find it. Good managers will also look for qualities that they like about the people around them—what they have in common can be used to build strong relationships.

No one is perfect. We all have strengths and weaknesses. Your attitude toward others will play a big part in whether you surround yourself with the right people. If you don't like the people around you, you might start by taking a looking at yourself.

14

WHERE THERE'S A WILL, THERE'S A WIN

Think positively

So much has been written about the power of positive thinking that it seems hardly necessary to mention it. Yet, much to my surprise, I constantly see negative thinking undermine people and hold them back. I have to conclude that these people haven't gotten the message or that they're just not paying attention.

However, when I started writing this, I realized that positive thinking isn't always enough. In addition to being positive, you must also be persistent. Being positive and persistent are inseparable—like success and me. Persistence is essential because you can't just start out being positive and then throw in the towel at the first sign of trouble. You have to stay positive because success rarely occurs overnight. Usually, overnight success stories are fables; they're simply not true. The fact that you just heard of someone today doesn't mean he or she hasn't been toiling away for decades.

When *The Apprentice* aired and immediately became a smash hit, I had over 30 years of experience to draw from for those boardroom scenes. It wasn't just a fluke or something new to me that I had to learn or fake. I knew what I was doing. Although I was new to television, the rest wasn't new to me; I had been making high-level executive decisions for more than 30 years.

Business is business, whether it's filmed or not. My business credentials and experience were the back-story for a television show based on a high-stakes New York corporation.

Thinking positively was important in my decision to make *The Apprentice.* When I was approached, I knew that doing the show could be risky, but I was positive that it would succeed. Had I chosen to listen to the arguments like "Most new television shows fail," "reality television is on the way out," and "you'll lose your credibility," I never would have done the show.

Instead, I asked myself positive questions:

- What if the show was a success?

- What if I enjoyed it?

- What if it proved to be enlightening?

- What if it brought The Trump Organization the recognition it deserved?

- What if the program proved to be a valuable stepping-stone to deserving candidates?

- What if the show helped the audience?

My long list of positives swamped the negatives.

Let the positive prevail by being positively persistent.

—Donald J. Trump

BE REALISTIC

I define myself as being cautiously positive. People who say, "You can do anything you want" are simply unrealistic. Some things are just not possible. For example, if I thought that today I could become an Olympic gold-medal swimmer, I'd need a shrink more than a swimming coach. No matter how many lessons I take, how hard I train, and how many steroids I consume, it won't happen, ever!

We all encounter roadblocks, obstacles that block our progress. But when we do, we have options if we remain positive. We can walk away, climb over, go under, or around them. We can also break through obstacles or have them demolished.

 MAKE IT HAPPEN IN YOUR LIFE

Make it a point to:

- Be positive every day. If you're not, no one will think you can succeed.

- Believe in yourself, exude confidence, and get in your competitors' way. Project yourself into their picture and upset their status quo.

- Break loose from your comfort zone by moving forward with the power and momentum that positive thinking creates.

- Zap negative thoughts and replace them with positive ones. Whatever energy you expend will build the positive stamina that is vital for success.

INSIST ON PERFECTION

For Trump National Golf Club in Briarcliff Manor, New York, I wanted to do something spectacular. I decided to erect a 110-foot waterfall that pumped 5,000 gallons of water per minute and cost $7 million to complete. The engineering and landscaping challenges were astounding. We had to move countless tons of earth and granite and encountered numerous setbacks before the water flowed.

If you think that building this waterfall was easy, or that it happened overnight, think again. During construction, I often felt like I was moving the granite myself. It was brutally hard work, but I remained positive. I refused to settle for anything less than I envisioned, and my positive perseverance worked.

Waterfall at Trump National Golf Club, Briarcliff Manor, New York.
Photo courtesy of the Trump Organization.

Ask Mr. Trump: Questions from Readers of the Trump University Blog

Q: How can I overcome my fear of cold calling and be myself instead of pretending to be someone else?

DJT: It really helps when you believe in what you're selling and when you have complete confidence in your knowledge of the product. To be a good salesperson, you must be positive about and absolutely convincing in your belief in your product. Be yourself, be totally prepared, and be positive.

15

Swim against the Tide

The comfort zone can pull you under

An old friend was working on Wall Street and not doing well. He looked worse—unhealthier and unhappier—each time I saw him, and it saddened me. I liked this guy, so I finally decided to tell him that he was beginning to look like a total loser. I hated speaking so harshly, but I really cared about him and wanted to help. When I asked him why he stayed on Wall Street, even though it obviously was not working for him, he explained that his family had always worked there and he felt obligated to continue the family tradition, even though it was killing him.

When I asked him what he liked to do, he told me he loved to tend the greens at his golf club. He knew golf courses, had a feel for them, and cared for them well. He also loved working outdoors and being in contact with people. I suggested that he look into the golf industry instead of continuing to suffer on Wall

Street. I also pointed out that his unhappiness was probably taking a heavy toll on his family.

Breaking away was difficult, but he made the move. He had to swim upstream, in hostile waters, and against the strongest tide—his family's and friends' traditions and expectations. He went into the golf business, where he became extremely successful. When I see him now, he's always beaming and looking healthy. He has a new lease on life and has become a different person because he had the guts to go against tradition, take control of his life, and change.

Your electricity might flow better through another socket.

—Donald J. Trump

COMFORT

It's easy to take the conventional route and not make waves, but the easiest way can be the mediocre way; it may be little more than just treading water. That's okay if you're content being comfortable and avoiding challenges, but it's not what I want from life. Most likely it isn't for you either, especially if you're reading this book.

Comfort can be a trickster that lures you into a false sense of security and leaves you stuck in the same old place. It can make you complacent and lazy and prevent you from getting ahead. Of course, there's a place for comfort. At times, it's what we all want. However, in the workplace, comfort will hold you back.

When you begin feeling comfortable, it should sound an alarm that alerts you that you might be falling into a trap. Ask yourself "Have I stopped moving or have I become stuck?"

When an employee told me, "I think it's good enough" in reference to an unfinished project, I fired him. Good enough? It wasn't good enough for me, and if it was good enough for him, he shouldn't be working for me. I want people who want more than good enough. I want employees who want great and will go the extra mile for the very best. I don't want to have to tell them; I want them to do it on their own.

 **Coach Trump** — MAKE IT HAPPEN IN YOUR LIFE

Don't be afraid to take risks, do what you love, and chart your own course. Here's what to do:

- Ask yourself whether you're doing what *you* want and what is right for you.

- Measure yourself against your feelings, ambition, needs, and goals, not those of others.

- Ignore the expectations of others. Stand up to your friends, family, teachers, colleagues, and those who think that they know what's best for you. Plug into your own energy.

BEWARE

A fine line exists between bravery and stupidity. Check out the tides, test the water, and know what you're getting into before you dive in.

Ask Mr. Trump: Questions from Readers of the Trump University Blog

Q: What is your advice for dealing with stress?

DJT: Stress frequently is related to focusing on problems, not solutions. If you put all your energy into the problem, you will have none left for the solution. Acknowledge the problem, and move on to things that are more positive.

One night in the early 1990s, when I was about a billion dollars in debt, I entered the conference room where my accountants were working. The mood was stressful. I decided to change the focus by describing my plans for some future projects and explaining how fantastic they would be. I painted vivid pictures of the success I saw. Although my accountants initially thought that I had flipped out from stress, my tactic worked. It changed our focus from agonizing over our big problem to looking at our future. Changing the focus was a turning point on my road back.

16

MONEY IS NOT ALWAYS THE BOTTOM LINE

It can be a scorecard, not the final score

I'm the last person you would expect to downplay the importance of money, since I've been fortunate to earn lots of it. People associate me with money, and it's given me a remarkable life. But making money should not be your primary purpose because if it is, you can end up with little else.

In reality, most of us need to make money; we have bills to pay. However, other objectives can be equally, or more, important, including the stimulation and satisfaction you receive from your work and its challenges. There's also the pleasure of helping others and doing good or the opportunity to learn, grow, and deal with outstanding people, to name just a few.

Think of your business career as a long-term venture that will occupy you for the rest of your life. Always build for tomorrow and consider objectives other than just the bucks. Think about building your long-term brand, your reputation, and your company. Make contacts and build relationships. Invest in the personal satisfactions that your work can bring you.

He that is of the opinion money will do everything may well be suspected of doing everything for money.

—Benjamin Franklin

If you're in business, making money must be part of the equation; profits keep business afloat. In our culture, the ability to earn money is the principle yardstick for measuring success. However, if how much you make is the whole enchilada, you could be making a serious mistake.

THE PAYOFF

I only go into deals when I like the subject and what I'm doing. I don't do deals strictly for money. If I get into a deal because there's something that I like, it turns out really well. I do things because I love them, and in the end, they make money. If I did things that I thought would make money but that I didn't like, I wouldn't do as well.

Think of money as part of your reward for succeeding. For me, money can't replace the exhilaration of working on exciting ventures, with amazing people, and in exotic places and achieving what most others wouldn't attempt. The money isn't what makes

INSIST ON PERFECTION

My first big deal was to transform the run-down Commodore Hotel into the beautiful Grand Hyatt Hotel. I didn't just want to make money, although that was definitely a part of my plan. I wanted to revitalize the dilapidated area around Grand Central Station and 42nd Street. The area had become a blight in the heart of midtown Manhattan—a corroded corridor through which millions of people passed. I wanted to create something wonderful for New York City and for everyone who lived in, worked in, and visited my city.

My success in transforming the Commodore Hotel began a renewal that continues today. Now the area is lively and bright. Yes, I made money, but there was more to it. Whenever I pass through the area, I feel a great sense of pride.

42nd Street Grand Central Station renovation.
Photo courtesy of the Trump Organization.

me build bigger, better, more beautifully, and create projects that get onlookers to stare in awe. The dollars can't compare to the sense of achievement that comes from seeing my buildings finally standing majestically in what once was a muddy hole.

I believe that if you remain true to your beliefs and work diligently, good things will occur. I was in the middle of my daily dealings when both *The Apprentice* and Trump University found their way to me. I didn't anticipate or look for either one, but here we are. Both are thriving and expanding in many ways, but I didn't get involved in them to make money.

 MAKE IT HAPPEN IN YOUR LIFE

Consider the importance of your life in terms of your contribution as well as your fulfillment:

- First ask yourself what you love to do, and then think about the money.

- Work on projects that you will be proud to be associated with and that will give you satisfaction. Make your work count on as many levels as you can, including giving to and helping others.

- View everything you do in terms of the big picture. See each step of a project not just as another task or job but also as a rung that will help you reach the next level in your life.

- Charge what you're worth. If you're good, ask for a fee that you deserve. Make your charges commensurate with the quality that you provide and try to be the most highly paid.

Trump International Hotel & Tower, Chicago.

A Very Special Week (Plus) in My Life . . .

Thursday

8:30 A.M. Rhona comes in to go over some scheduling for May—even though it is only March. May 1 will be the Costume Institute Ball at the Metropolitan Museum of Art. This is a wonderful event because of Anna Wintour's fine work for one thing. This month, I will also do an interview regarding the United Nations, and one for CNN *en Español*. I review invitations and interview requests.

9:00 A.M. George Ross comes in to talk about Avon, which has space in Trump Tower and a storefront on Fifth Avenue.

9:30 A.M. I take a call from Bob Wright, one of the all-time business greats and an equally great person. He and his wife Suzanne will be joining us for dinner next week.
    Oprah's team calls in, and I agree to do a segment for *Oprah* to be filmed in my apartment.

10:00 A.M. Jay Bienstock, of Mark Burnett Productions and executive producer of *The Apprentice,* calls to confirm the final casting call for the next *Apprentice* to be held in Los Angeles on May 11. We discuss the show and some points that need to be finalized.

10:30 A.M. Cathy Glosser comes in to discuss the Marcraft cocktail party later this spring and to set up a fragrance meeting with William Lauder and Steven Florio at Estee Lauder. My suits, ties, and fragrance have done well.

Donald J. Trump
Signature Collection

Donald J. Trump
Signature Watch Collection

Donald J. Trump
Signature Tie Collection

11:00 A.M. Rhona comes in to confirm a board dinner at Sparks Steakhouse that sounds like a good idea. I remember to call Jean Georges to order a bottle of champagne for Robert and Kim Kiyosaki and their partner Sharon Lechter because they will be making their first visit to the restaurant. I recommend Jean Georges to anyone who likes the best cuisine available; it's always terrific, but it is not easy to get reservations.

Don Jr. and Ivanka come in to discuss more details on the Trump Ocean Club in Panama. This will be a beautiful building, resembling a sail, and the environment is ideal. We also review the May 4 grand opening date of Trump Tower in Philadelphia.

Rhona comes in to tell us that the *20/20* segment with Don Jr. and Ivanka is scheduled to air on May 5. Seems like May is in the air and it's still only March, but we always have to plan ahead. Rhona has also confirmed an *Avenue* magazine shoot with Don Jr. and Ivanka in May. It's a good thing my kids have a great deal of energy because they have very full schedules themselves, with quite a bit of international travel.

12:00 P.M. Andy Weiss comes in to go over more buyouts concerning the Trump International Hotel & Tower in Chicago. We should be ready to go by the end of the year on this project, if not sooner. I've always liked Chicago and have enjoyed this project.

I call Melania to see how she's doing. She's feeling fine and is very busy with the details that go along with preparing for a new arrival.

12:30 P.M. I take and make a few calls, and I ask for the rest of the messages that came in during my meetings. I ask Chris Devine to send me up some lunch from the Trump Tower grill, the DT burger sounds good.

Rhona comes in to go over some requests, and I agree to do a Lefrak Organization video regarding the anniversary of Newport, and an Italian *Vogue* magazine photo shoot.

It's a beautiful day today and I decide I should take a drive to the Trump National Golf Club in Briarcliff, New York, so I cancel my lunch here and I'll have lunch there instead. Then I do a property check so I can see the grounds and the villas and see what improvements are under way. It's looking great for the upcoming golf season.

In May we'll have The Spring Fashion Show which will benefit the American Cancer Society and breast cancer research. I go over the plans and it should be a great success.

5:00 P.M. I'm back in the office and returning calls, then Bernie Diamond comes in to give me an update on several issues, and I ask Allen Weisselberg to come in as well. These guys are focused and thorough.

I agree to do an interview for Michael Douglas later this spring for a celebrity golf event he's doing at Trump National Golf Club in Los Angeles. I would like to play in it but I have a scheduling conflict that I can't change.

I take a call from Jeff Zucker at NBC, and we conference in Mark Burnett.

5:45 P.M. Rhona gives me the daily mail. It includes more requests and invitations, documents, and a bundle of magazines. I spend about 45 minutes with this pile, making some notes and organizing a pile for tomorrow. There's a letter from someone who would like to make Trumpernickel bread instead of the usual pumpernickel variety.

6:30 P.M. I turn out the lights in my office and head home.

17

LEARNING IS EXCITING

Each new project is an adventure

To erect a building in New York City, a developer must know thousands of things about zoning, air rights, tax laws, and how to deal with contractors, architects, unions, and city hall to name a few. Believe me, you can't become a successful developer overnight because there is a huge amount to learn first. To me, this is an adventure.

Whenever I start something new, I know I have tons to learn. I see each new project as a blank page that I can't wait to fill. I get excited because I love to investigate, dig in new areas, acquire information, put it together, and gain an in-depth understanding of something completely new.

I've had this feeling at every stage of my career; it's how I begin every successful project. I consider it a sign; if I don't feel excited, I usually pass on the opportunity, even if it could produce huge profits. My enthusiasm drives me to learn, and what I learn gives me more control. My knowledge also helps me avoid mistakes and eliminate problems that could arise. I studied up on travel before starting GoTrump.com, my travel agency. I studied the men's fashion industry for my Donald J. Trump Signature Collection of menswear. I researched and read carefully before starting Trump University; and that's just to name a few examples.

When I started as coproducer of *The Apprentice*, I knew a little about the entertainment industry, but I knew nothing in-depth about reality television. So I had to learn: I read, spoke with experts, paid attention, listened, and applied everything I learned. It was like taking a series of crash courses. Although it was new, it was fascinating. Since I had jumped in the deep end, I knew I'd better learn how to swim, which I did. It was, and continues to be, a great experience.

REMAIN OPEN

There is only one thing I know, and that is I know nothing.

—Socrates

Remain open to new ideas and information. Nobody knows it all and thinking that you do is dumb; it can slam the door on great discoveries and opportunities. If I had started in business thinking that I knew everything, I'd have been finished before I began. Don't make that mistake. Every business has surprises, hidden dangers beneath the surface, and simple problems that become complex.

In my life, I want each day to be full of discoveries, and I frequently wonder what I'll be learning each day. It's a terrific way to

Donald J. Trump Signature Suit Collection.
Photo courtesy of the Trump Organization.

start the day. When I learn, it makes me feel great, alive, and excited—it makes me want to learn more. As a result, I'm never bored, which I think is a big reason for my success.

Never think of learning as a burden or a chore. It may require some discipline, but it can be a stimulating and exciting adventure.

 MAKE IT HAPPEN IN YOUR LIFE

- Become a perpetual student; gobble up information on many subjects.

- Periodically ask yourself, "What should I learn more about?" Take inventory and study areas in which you may be weak or may wish to investigate. Look into topics that you always avoided or those that are outside your area of expertise. Every day, I try to read newspapers, like the *Financial Times*, because it's important to my business to know what's going on worldwide, but I also love to read golf magazines.

BEWARE

Nothing turns people off more than a person who constantly needs to demonstrate how much he or she knows. Before long, people stop listening, but they never forget when someone is such a bore.

18

SEE THE
WHOLE PICTURE

But be prepared for the picture to change

Some people have tunnel vision. When they look, they see only certain parts of the picture, not the entire picture. When you're passionate or intensely focused, it's easy to miss what's directly in front of you or misinterpret what you see. When you don't see the whole picture, you are more likely to head in the wrong direction; make mistakes; and waste your time, energy, and resources.

Avoid this by calling on your team—key employees, advisors, friends, and mentors. Your team can help you see the whole picture. They may have expertise, insights, or sensibilities that you lack. Surround yourself with top people, enlist their input, and listen to their advice.

A group of businesspeople proposed building an atrium on the ground floor of 40 Wall Street. According to their vision, people would enter the building and find themselves in a verdant wonderland, an oasis that would be a sharp contrast to the hustle, bustle, concrete, and skyscrapers outside. Their basic idea was to transform 40 Wall Street into the downtown equivalent of Trump Tower, except they missed a critical piece: The steel columns that support the 72-story building could not be altered or removed. The businesspeople were so excited about the idea of the atrium that they completely overlooked the fact that the building's major structural component was in the way.

EVERYTHING CHANGES

Much of life and business is about survival, and Darwin taught us that to survive, we must adapt. Evolution is constant in business and life. Even the most powerful empires have come and gone. Just look at history, the Roman, Ottoman, and British Empires once dominated the world, and then each faded away.

Anticipate change and embrace it; change can affect the entire picture. Recognize new developments that you can capitalize on, profit from, and use to open new doors.

—Donald J. Trump

Since everything always changes, constantly reevaluate the big picture. Reexamine the landscape; see what's changed and what those differences could mean to you. Then figure out how you can keep up with and make the changes work for you. When

I realized how fast the world is moving, I faced the choice of adapting or losing out. I decided to adapt by increasing my work hours. It wasn't a big sacrifice because I love what I do, and I've always been a hard worker. Since I boosted my workload, I'm happier and more productive than ever. And those who want to compete with me have to keep up. Always move forward or you'll be left with crumbs, not pie.

I see my business, the Trump Organization, as a living organism that continually evolves. Like most large companies, my company consists of many parts that must be closely coordinated to operate at peak performance. So it's up to me to understand the big picture and how the business environment is changing. I have to make sure that all the ingredients are present; that all the parts are well oiled, fully operational, and ready to go; and that each segment has whatever it needs in terms of people, time, and resources to deliver products worthy of the Trump name.

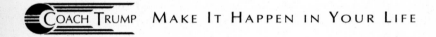 COACH TRUMP　MAKE IT HAPPEN IN YOUR LIFE

Here's how to see the big picture and adapt to changes:

- Make it your goal to create a business that will be a huge success for many years.

- Strengthen your weaknesses, fill in your gaps, and explore new areas. But don't neglect or let your existing strengths erode.

- Don't be stagnant, complacent, or rest on your laurels, no matter how successful you've been. Giving 50 percent is not enough; your clients and customers deserve more—they deserve your best.

Ask Mr. Trump: Questions from Readers of the Trump University Blog

Q: I'm in an MBA program and currently in a leadership class where, for our final project, we have to prepare a presentation about a leader we admire. My group has chosen you, and we would like to know what qualities you think are essential for a strong leader.

DJT:

- Leadership is not a group effort. If you're in charge, then be in charge.

- Be focused. Every day put everything you've got into what you do.

- Trust your instincts.

- Maintain your momentum, and keep everyone moving forward.

- Believe in yourself. If you don't, no one else will.

- Be tenacious and tough. Don't give up.

- See yourself as victorious and leading a winning team.

- Live on the edge. Don't let yourself become complacent.

- Be passionate about what you do. Without passion, you'll never be an effective leader.

- Think big and win big.

19

Wait for the Right Pitch

*Business success is all about
patience and timing*

Timing is everything. Products are now rushed to market at record speed, often before they're ready, so companies can make a big splash and cash in quickly. If companies wait, they know that a competitor might produce the same item faster, cheaper, or better. So the product is rushed to market.

However, good timing involves more than just being first. It's also about choosing the right opportunities. In business, the main objective is to produce a string of hits and have your company survive. Although speed is tempting because it can mean big and quick profits, it can also cause early exits. So wait for the right deal; think about the long term, which requires planning, patience, and discipline.

Over the years, I've watched and played lots of tennis, and I've been fascinated by the remarkable timing of the best players.

When the best players approach the ball, they stay continuously focused, like big cats waiting for the precise moment to strike. When the time is right, they lash out with all their power and strength. The sound of a racket hitting the ball is electric; it thrills the crowd.

Comics are also masters of timing, using pauses, shrugs, gestures, looks, glances, walks, and movements to make us laugh. Without uttering a single word, they can have you laughing hysterically. It's a major part of their art.

When I'm in negotiations, especially if I really want something, I often use timing to get an edge. One of my tactics is to lay back and act as if I'm not sure whether I want the deal or not. This throws off the competition and gives me more time to assess exactly what I want and how to get it. When I hold back, I ask myself, "Why do I want this deal?" "How much do I want it?" "What is motivating me?"

Interestingly, my answers to these questions usually help me determine if, when, and how I should make my move. Waiting

Donald J. Trump playing tennis at the Mar-a-Lago club, Palm Beach, Florida.
Photo courtesy of the Trump Organization.

also helps you organize your plans, set priorities, and be less impulsive, eager, and emotional.

I wait until the ball is in my court before I swing, which gives me the best chance of making my point.

—Donald J. Trump

LEARN TO BE PATIENT

If during negotiations you seem overly eager or show your hand too soon, the price can skyrocket and the terms can change. Impatience can give the other side the upper hand, which usually makes it harder to strike a deal. Your impatience can force you to pay a hefty premium that could sap profits from the venture.

Frequently, when you really want a deal, the conditions aren't right. Essential pieces may not be available at that time. Fortunately, things change and that's where patience really pays. For some projects, I've waited up to 30 years until all my requirements could be met and for others, I'm still waiting. I do not know when the conditions will change for them to work or if they ever will change.

I was interested in investing in a large piece of real estate, but something or other always came up that kept me from making the final move. As these problems continued, I started feeling uneasy and decided to wait. A few months later, a huge storm struck and severely damaged the area. It destroyed any possibility that I could develop the project I had intended for that land. My decision to wait saved me a fortune. The land may have been great, but the timing was all wrong.

Waiting can be harder than moving forward, and it sure takes more discipline. You have to control your instincts and emotions and keep yourself in check, which isn't easy. But when the terms aren't right, stand firm, be strong, and don't give in. Try to get better terms, but if you can't, walk away or wait.

I'm a big believer in momentum, but at certain times, you must slow down the pace. Being methodical isn't necessarily being complacent—it's part of a technique. If you don't reduce the speed, you run the risk of spinning out of control, going off course, and placing yourself in danger.

Control the tempo and you can usually control the game. When you play at your tempo, you're in charge. Others must respond to you when you set the agenda and the speed at which the game runs, which increases your chances of winning.

20

AVOID FIXED PATTERNS

Be open and flexible

When I was building Trump Tower, I planned to call it Tiffany Tower because it is next to the landmark Tiffany & Co. store on Fifth Avenue in New York City. Then a friend asked why I would name my building after a famous jewelry store when it was my building. He made a good point, so I changed the name to Trump Tower. Now, Trump Tower has become a celebrated site in its own right—a destination and a name that people recognize. It pays to listen and to be willing to change.

At times, you must be obstinate and tough or business predators will eat you alive. However, you must also know when to change and be flexible. If you insist on following fixed patterns, it can limit you and your future. Everything changes and virtually nothing goes according to plan. So when changes occur, as they will, you must adapt, change, and even make U-turns.

Trump Tower, Fifth Avenue.
Photo courtesy of the Trump Organization.

BE AWARE OF YOUR COMFORT ZONE

Don't get too secure in your comfort zone. When you get too comfortable, you can become complacent and never grow or broaden your experiences. Staying put may give you a secure life, but it can also be dull, stagnant, and unproductive. Take the challenge; invite change into your life and business.

Success is good. Success with significance is even better.

—Donald J. Trump

INSIST ON PERFECTION

When *The Apprentice* was nominated for an Emmy Award as the best reality show of 2005, I attended the ceremonies in Los Angeles. As part of the entertainment, the producers asked me to sing the theme song from *Green Acres* with Megan Mullally while I wore overalls and a straw hat and held a pitchfork. Now, this was a stretch for me, completely out of character, but I agreed because I knew it would be fun, even though I have never mistaken myself for Elvis or Pavarotti.

Donald J. Trump with Megan Mullally at the Emmy Awards.
Photo courtesy of NBC Universal.

Throughout my performance, my focus was on building good will for *The Apprentice*. While singing and dressing in costume are clearly not what I do, I took the challenge and gave everyone a good laugh. It was terrific fun, everyone loved it, and we got wonderful press. Surprisingly, I even won the talent award that night.

If I had not been flexible or a good sport, I would have missed a golden opportunity to have fun, amuse others, and create some buzz. I enjoyed getting out of character, doing something different, surprising people, and making them laugh. Don't be inflexible and let great chances pass you by.

Success can be achieved in numerous ways. Some people never vary; they take the straightest, most direct route. Others meander, traveling circuitous routes that may not be easily understood. Break your patterns; try new ways. Staying in your comfort zone may limit your understanding.

Before *The Apprentice*, I received several proposals for reality shows, but I found none appealing. When Mark Burnett approached me, I could have immediately declined because I figured that I would not like his proposal any more than the others I had received. But I remained open, listened to him, and realized that I liked his idea. I was flexible when I could have remained closed, and look how fabulously it turned out. I'm glad I kept an open mind and a positive attitude.

Life is filled with so much that we can't control, like natural catastrophes, terrorist attacks, wars, accidents, and illness. Don't be so rigid that you can be broken. It's wiser to be pliable and to adapt to whatever comes along.

 MAKE IT HAPPEN IN YOUR LIFE

Any new action can bring strength. Adaptation is an old theory but it's a solid one.

- Understand that life is unpredictable and that things will change. Realize that your methods and goals must change for you to keep pace and succeed.

- Keep abreast of what's happening around the globe. See how you can integrate recent developments into your world. They can open the door to new interests and excitement.

- Be willing to move out of your comfort zone and try new things. Take some chances, be daring, and embrace the new.

- Always be open; listen attentively and be willing to change. Change isn't an admission that you were wrong or a sign of defeat; it's frequently a smart thing to do.

Ask Mr. Trump: Questions from Readers of the Trump University Blog

Q: Short of firing people, how do you fix a team that is broken?

DJT: Try to mix up the team. Add and subtract members until you get a group that works well together. Excessive egos can disrupt a team. A weak leader could be a more effective follower and not everyone can be in charge. Try to balance the team and avoid weak links and Napoleons. Team members should be able to change roles and adapt to tasks without undue resistance or difficulty.

A Very Special Week (Plus) in My Life . . .

Friday

8:30 A.M. I call Ashley Cooper about my trip to Scotland in April. Scotland is the birthplace of golf, and it makes sense to develop a course there. My mother's family came from Scotland, so I have roots there.

9:00 A.M. Rhona lets me know that the American Art Award black-tie gala at the Whitney Museum later this spring will honor Federated and its chairman Terry Lundgren, so I will be attending. She also tells me the copy machine has been fixed—again—and it is actually working. Things are looking up.

9:30 A.M. I have a meeting with Jill Cremer about the Canouan Island project in the Grenadines, another beautiful location.
My accounting team, Allen, Jeff, and Eric, come in for a meeting. I ask Thuy Nguyen for a copy of the proposed Los Angeles *Apprentice* schedule.

10:00 A.M. I talk to Jeff Zucker about the NBC Primetime Review that is scheduled for mid-May at Radio City Music Hall. That will be a dynamic industry day.
I go over the entertainment schedule at the Trump Taj Mahal in Atlantic City, New Jersey. Andrea Bocelli will be appearing in June, and we will have a tribute to Andrea at Daniel, a well known restaurant in New York City.
I talk to Mike Donovan, my pilot, about my trip to Scotland, and we decide to pick up Melania's parents in Slovenia for the trip back to the United States.

11:00 A.M. I take a call from Craig Plestis of NBC, and then one from Jim Dowd. Jim tells me about a *GQ* magazine interview request for May, which I decide to do.

Rhona comes in and we finalize my travel plans to Canouan Island sometime in late May.

Sonja Talesnik comes in to go over some developments at Trump World Tower. I ask if she's been to Megu, a fantastic Japanese restaurant, and advise her to go.

12:00 P.M.   I ask Chris Devine to send up some lunch, and I go over some of the piles of mail that have been brought in. I receive many invitations, even from people I don't know, but it's good to be wanted.

George Ross stops by. We discuss Asprey and wonder why they changed their signature shopping bag. It was elegant and recognizable, much like the Tiffany gift bag. Marketing carries a strong message, especially when the brand is top level, and it can be a mistake to change it.

1:00 P.M.   Jason Greenblatt comes in with some documents for me to sign, and we discuss a few licensing issues about the Canouan Island project.

1:30 P.M.   I return some calls and review some documents. The phones are a form of music after a while, and it's a familiar hum in this office. Once we counted an average of 400 calls a day to my office—some days more, some days less. I think today is one of the *more* days considering the number of calls I have to return.

2:30 P.M.   I take a call from Mark Burnett. Looks like we'll have the season finale of *The Apprentice* in Los Angeles, California, this June. I'll be in Los Angeles to film the next season anyway starting this June.

Matthew Calamari stops by and gives me some updates regarding properties, and we talk about the upcoming baseball season for a few minutes. Not too many people know this, but I was a good baseball player. I've always remained interested in the sport, as George Steinbrenner knows.

3:00 P.M. I ask Rhona to get my mail and documents ready for the plane. I will do more work on the flight down to Palm Beach, Florida. I review my weekend itinerary briefly, and I ask Thuy Nguyen, an assistant, to call Allen Weisselberg to come in for a meeting.

3:25 P.M. I leave the office with Keith Schiller, and Eddie Diaz drives us to the airport.

4:00 P.M. It's wheels up at 4:00 P.M. as I leave New York City in my jet for Palm Beach. I am hosting the great Elton John, and I will be in the audience tomorrow night for his concert at Mar-a-Lago.

21

SPEED KILLS—THE COMPETITION

Get right to the point

Unfortunately, I'm frequently on the receiving end of conversations with people who don't edit their thoughts before speaking. As they ramble, I think to myself, "How long are they going to take to get to the point? We could've flown to Australia by now, and they're still taking off."

Business is no place for stream-of-consciousness babbling, no matter how colorfully you think you speak. Whatever you do, keep it short, fast, and right to the point. Being concise is polite; it shows that you respect other people's time. When most folks have to listen to endless discourses, they squirm, their minds wander, or they frequently don't listen. Instead of making their points, long-winded talkers turn off their audiences.

Before I went into partnership with the Brazilian entrepreneur Ricardo Bellino in Trump Realty Brazil, which will be the largest golf and residential complex in Latin America, I gave him only three minutes to explain his idea. I was extremely busy and not eager to listen to a presentation. So I expected him to decline. Not only did Ricardo accept my terms, he made such a great presentation in the allotted time that I was fascinated with the deal. Now we're partners. It's amazing what people can do when they have deadlines.

Give yourself deadlines. Practice delivering your presentation in less than five minutes, and then chop it to three minutes. Anything longer can seem like a lecture. Edit yourself by cutting everything that isn't absolutely necessary. The people you speak to will be grateful that you distilled your pitch to its essence. If they have questions, they'll ask, which is what you want.

Extraneous information in long-winded presentations is like junk mail. Everyone hates junk mail, especially busy people. No one wants to sort through irrelevant stuff. Instead of delivering verbal junk, limit your pitch to only necessary information.

If you can't write your idea on the back of my calling card, you don't have a clear idea.

—David Belasco

Trump Jet.
Photo courtesy of the Trump Organization.

BUSINESS IS A RELAY RACE

Business is like a relay race. All team members must be fast, focused, and able to coordinate with each other. Each member has to know how to run with and pass the baton. No runner can lag behind or the entire team will suffer.

I once hired a very qualified young man who I expected to be great. Boy, was I ever wrong. This guy took so long to explain everything that I began to dread talking with him. He was just too slow. Yes, he was thorough and painstaking, but he couldn't keep pace. He wasted too much time. I had to let him go because he couldn't adapt to the environment and keep up.

Someone who analyzed my negotiating technique concluded that I had an advantage because I got to the point faster than anyone else. He said that while my adversaries were formulating their sentences, I had finished writing the book. I cut straight to the point because, before I speak, I map out the deal in my mind. I know the deal inside and out. I understand exactly what I need, what I want, how I want to proceed, and how far I'll go.

I didn't develop that ability overnight; I've worked at it for years. Once you start editing yourself, the process moves into other areas of your life. Before long, it spills over to virtually everything from relaying messages to writing letters, e-mail, or reports to ordering lunch.

When you watch *The Apprentice*, notice how candidates who present facts most succinctly stand out. Nobody wants to listen to five-minute explanations that could have been said in 15 to 20 seconds. Long speeches are a red flag to my advisors and me. We don't have time for verbose dialogues, and we won't hire people who can't promptly make their points.

 **MAKE IT HAPPEN IN YOUR LIFE**

Identify your interests and those of the listener. Limit your conversation to what is necessary at that moment. Be discerning.

- Plan what you want to say before you speak.

- Learn to read your audience. When people lose interest, they give signs, so watch your audience carefully. As soon as you see their attention wander, wrap up your point and move on to the next.

BEWARE

Brevity is important, but do not shorten information to the point that you become unclear. In communications, clarity is always the top priority. Clarity and brevity aren't incompatible, but the combination can take thought and practice to master.

Ask Mr. Trump: Questions from Readers of the Trump University Blog

Q: I read your testimony to Congress on the United Nations renovation project. It was simple to understand and didn't slip into jargon or manager-speak. Why do you think people use jargon when simple words will do?

DJT: I've noticed that insecure people are often long-winded when they try to convince others that they are important or have special knowledge. I believe in getting to the point in the most direct way possible. It saves everyone's time and teaches you to distill information into sound bites that cannot be misinterpreted. I move quickly in business, so I don't have the time, the desire, or the need to pontificate or sound important. Oftentimes, this backfires. Being concise is more effective, but not necessarily easier.

Sometimes I ask people to explain things to me in less than three sentences to make sure they've got it down. Condensing your thoughts is a great technique for both speaking and writing. Busy people work in sound bites; anything more can be a waste of time or cause confusion. I prefer to speak simply and clearly whether I'm addressing my employees or Congress.

22

DO MORE—ALWAYS DO MORE

Constantly try to top yourself

Lots of people are unable to motivate themselves; they don't know how to move themselves into a position to succeed. I believe that success starts with your attitude: You must be convinced that you will succeed. When you think that nothing can stop you, others will adopt your view. They will support you, jump on your bandwagon, and contribute to your success. They will give you help that they won't provide to those who they don't believe in themselves.

Learn to project a winning, confident attitude that inspires success. Begin by working with your internal processes; for example, how you greet each day. Before you get out of bed, take a few moments to welcome the day. Think of the reasons why today can be special or important for your future. Say aloud to yourself, "What a great day!" Think about how you can make wonderful things happen.

As ideas flow through your mind, feel the enthusiasm that your positive attitude has generated and the smile on your face.

You'll be amazed at how energetic it will make you feel; that energy will carry you through the day and help you to be happier and more productive.

No person who is enthusiastic about his work has anything to fear from life.

—Samuel Goldwyn

CHALLENGE YOURSELF

I thrive on challenges—on doing what others think cannot be done. I use challenges for self-motivation. To me, the best challenges are the ones I give myself. At this point in my life, I don't need to impress anyone, but I still need to satisfy my own goals and become involved in things that excite me.

After Trump Tower was completed and hailed as such a rousing success, I knew it was just the beginning. I wanted more; I needed to become involved in larger scale projects. So I built Trump World Tower at the United Nations Plaza. This 72-story

Trump World Tower and United Nations Plaza.
Photo courtesy of the Trump Organization.

skyscraper is the world's largest residential structure and the world's 48th tallest building. It's a magnificent building in midtown Manhattan, near the East River, and it has been a sensational success. Most of all, it stands as a monument to what can be achieved when you try to outdo your best.

Now, I'm about to build a 50-story hotel in Dubai, in the United Arab Emirates, one of the world's fastest growing cities.

Dubai Rendering.
Photo courtesy of the Trump Organization.

This magnificent structure will feature two elegant arches that will come together at the upper portion of the hotel. It's my first venture in the Middle East. And here's another first for me, the hotel will sit on a man-made island.

Compete with yourself. Don't be a one-hit wonder. After you succeed, find ways to surpass what you've already done. I'm convinced whatever I do, I can always do something bigger and better. I avoid complacency by always trying to reach new heights with bigger and better results. Being satisfied can undermine you and keep you from reaching your potential.

When I was asked to host *Saturday Night Live*, the last thing I needed was more exposure because I was already well known. However, appearing on the legendary show presented me with a new and totally different challenge. Although I wasn't a seasoned performer, I saw no reason to decline an opportunity to have fun, meet great people, and enjoy a new experience. And I had a ball!

As you may know, in the early 1990s, I had some financial troubles. In fact, I was $9 billion in debt. I know that this

Donald J. Trump hosting *Saturday Night Live*.
Photo courtesy of NBC Universal.

amount of indebtedness would have crushed most people, but it made me determined to fight back. I took an attitude check and resolved to remain positive about my circumstances. I knew the conditions would change for the better, and they certainly have.

It took a lot of effort to weather that storm, but I did it. I honestly believe that my attitude, willingness to work hard, and determination pulled me through. Things are so much better now than they were back then, and I came out of it better than I had been at my previous best.

The most important lesson I learned from that ordeal was that I could handle pressure. At that time, many of my friends also fell deeply in debt. Some went bankrupt and are no longer forces in the business. Despite my tremendous debt and all the pressure, I never went bankrupt. I was able to work it out, and I learned I could take the heat. You don't know what pressure is until you owe billions of dollars to banks and they all want their money at once.

 MAKE IT HAPPEN IN YOUR LIFE

Always strive for more. Realize there are tremendous opportunities available to you, and be alert to them.

- Never be satisfied. Don't rest on your achievements. Do more, be more, and give more. Avoid becoming complacent because of your accomplishments.

- Start every day with a sense of appreciation and excitement about what you can achieve. Think of how you can accomplish your goals.

- Find challenges that will improve you, your business, and your life.

- Generously reward people who help you succeed. Thank and compensate them. Find meaningful ways to show your appreciation. Never take help for granted. Take good care of those who help you, and they will take good care of you.

BEWARE

Be confident and project self-assurance, but don't get carried away. Make sure that you don't come across as arrogant, cocky, or overly impressed with yourself. Those traits quickly alienate and turn people off.

23

LEADERS SET THE PACE

Find your working tempo

Running a business is like being an orchestra conductor. When you lead an organization or a business, you, like a conductor, must take charge and exercise control. How well your people perform is your responsibility; direction flows from the top, and you're the maestro.

When the orchestra plays, the maestro maintains the tempo. Imagine if each orchestra member set his or her own pace and played at his or her own speed. It would be a cacophony, an ear-shattering mess, a disaster. When a business doesn't follow a steady tempo, it can also create chaos.

I'm the conductor who leads the Trump Organization; I set the tempo. In my organization, I set a rapid pace, which is called allegro in symphonic circles. I pay close attention to tempo because I know that it's vital to keep the momentum going at all times. I provide strong leadership, and, at times, this can be hard and not what I want to do. However, that's my job. My team looks to me for direction, taking my cues and following my lead.

Effective leaders develop individual tempos and utilize them. Your tempo is like an inner metronome that constantly keeps time. It should never stop—even when the world is exploding around you. The people you work with will feel your tempo and plug into it. When they do, everyone will work better together and enjoy it more.

I'm often asked, "What makes you tick?" I simply respond, "My own tempo, which is fast." We each have our own internal tempos that govern how quickly we move. It's an integral, distinguishing part of us. Some people are deliberate, contemplative, and reflective. Others, like me, proceed at lightning speed. I think that my speed enables me to do more. It also challenges my people to keep up with me.

When I'm making deals, I'm in the zone. The tempo is music that makes me feel like I can't lose.

—Donald J. Trump

When I conduct a meeting, I need those present to keep up with me, to be on the same page. The people who work with me know my pace, and they've adjusted to it. My employees know that I like to work quickly, so they prepare for meetings. We don't waste time, so we move rapidly at my speed.

BE IN THE ZONE

I'm sure you've heard people say that they're in "the zone." What they mean is that they've reached a certain level of performance where everything comes naturally, easily, and seems to flow. Something inside takes over and sweeps them up. They operate at their best.

When I'm making deals, I'm in the zone. Innately, instinctively all the pieces seem to fall in place, and I know exactly what to say and when and how forcefully to say it. I know the steps that need to be taken and how the next step should proceed. When this occurs, I know that I'm working at my best level. I feel that I am doing what I was born to do, and that life is exciting and uplifting—a feeling I savor and try to repeat.

Remember when you had to write term papers. Sometimes it was murder to get started, so you did everything imaginable other than sit down and actually write. When there was no more time to kill, you finally started to work. Surprisingly, something changed. You found that it wasn't so hard, the words began to flow, and you were getting your thoughts across. You were producing pages without much pain. You got into a zone; you found your tempo and flow.

 MAKE IT HAPPEN IN YOUR LIFE

If you think your tempo is too slow, here are tips to speed it up:

- Look at yourself; see what tempo is natural to you. Become aware of that tempo and how well it works for you.

- Decide if you're satisfied with your tempo or if you should speed it up or slow it down. Identify additional items that you could accomplish or do better if you changed your pace.

- Plan how you can demonstrate your new tempo to your people without putting them in shock. Perhaps, you could move in increments instead of changing the tempo all at once.

- Monitor your organization and determine how well everyone keeps up. Learn the cause of bottlenecks and try to clear them up. Then, when everyone is up to speed, see if you can change it again.

24

RESULTS MATTER MORE than ROUTES

Let people follow their own paths

A copywriter was sitting at his desk, staring out the window and making absolutely no attempt to look busy, which drove his coworkers crazy. So they complained to the boss who asked them how long the copywriter had been behaving that way. When they told him, the boss instructed them to get the copywriter coffee, lunch, or anything his heart desired and to make sure that he wasn't interrupted. When the coworkers complained, the boss explained, "The last few times time he acted like this, he came up with ideas that were worth millions of dollars. So whatever you do, don't disturb him; let him create!"

Everyone works differently; we all take different paths and use diverse methods. Some deliberate endlessly and then move suddenly to complete a task. Others make an immediate decision and then take forever to implement it. Frequently, the results are the same; it's just a matter of style.

INSIST ON PERFECTION

If people examined how I work, they would probably report, "He spends most of his time on the phone." True, I talk on the phone constantly. That's how I do business, and I find it to be efficient. I'm not just chatting with friends all day; I'm putting deals together and conducting important business. I get a lot accomplished on the phone. That's my style. If you want to say that all I do is have daily chat fests, it's fine with me. For me, my way has been highly productive.

Donald J. Trump on top of Trump World Tower Construction.
Photo courtesy of the Trump Organization.

Be nonjudgmental. See and record the facts without coloring them.

—Donald J. Trump

I don't mind working hard, but I see absolutely no reason to work stupidly. Working stupidly is not making a full effort, not trying to perform at your best. Not really trying cheats you and everyone you work with. For example, some people put more effort into looking busy than they would if they actually tried to do a bang-up job. Their approach is just plain stupid because, invariably, their bosses or coworkers will catch on. When the sham is revealed, people will resent being deceived. They will feel ripped off and take it personally, as they should. The faker showed that he or she didn't really care about them, the company, or the team.

EXAMINE YOUR HABITS

We all form habits and fall into certain patterns. If you consistently try to produce work that meets the highest standard, that's more important than how you go about achieving it. Your pattern may be based on integrity and the desire to always provide the best, which is definitely a good approach.

Review your habits and make sure that they are taking you in the right direction. Are your habits consistent with your ambitions and values? Are they providing the results you want and producing them in the right way?

I was once told that the clearest way to see people and events is to examine them nonjudgmentally—to see and record the facts without coloring them with a "this is right" or "that is wrong" attitude. This follows a journalistic approach in its purest sense—news without a slant. A nonjudgmental approach collects and reports the facts without jumping to conclusions or interpreting their meaning. This approach may require you to do a little more thinking, which can only be a good thing.

Never presume that your way is the only way, whether you're talking about work, ethics, or politics. Be tolerant of diverse opinions, practices, and views. Be grateful for the diversity in our lives and for the benefits of being exposed to so many different backgrounds and beliefs. Take the time to try to understand other viewpoints—how and why those people feel and act as they do. Gather information, get the whole story, and don't jump to conclusions or judge.

Results are what matter; the rest is style. Thomas Edison remarked that he knew a lot about results because he found several thousand things that didn't work on his way to finding something that did.

 **COACH TRUMP** MAKE IT HAPPEN IN YOUR LIFE

Here are suggestions to improve your work habits:

- Find your most effective way to work. Do you work better in the mornings, or when you sleep late? Examine your habits, patterns, and comfort zones. Try to develop an objective understanding of how you act.

- Learn what changes you should make. Are any of your habits, patterns, or approaches holding you back and keeping you from advancing to the next level? If so, identify and fix them so you can move on.

A Very Special Week (Plus) in My Life . . .

Saturday

I played a great golf game, which always puts me in a better-than-ever humor. (Golf is a brain game, and when I do well, it's a great feeling.) I checked out the course and made sure everything was perfect. I also visited the site of the concert to see how things are going; it looked like they were ready for a big night.

What can I say? Elton John is one of the great entertainers of all time. He sang for two hours, just himself and the piano. He had the entire audience (which was packed in) mesmerized. He's not only a great talent but also a great person. I'm honored to call him my friend.

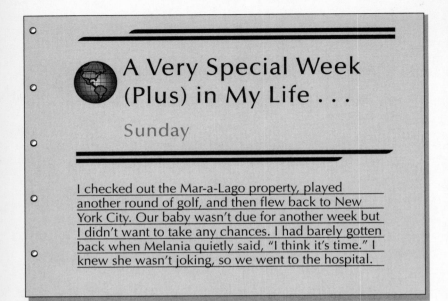

A Very Special Week (Plus) in My Life . . .

Sunday

I checked out the Mar-a-Lago property, played another round of golf, and then flew back to New York City. Our baby wasn't due for another week but I didn't want to take any chances. I had barely gotten back when Melania quietly said, "I think it's time." I knew she wasn't joking, so we went to the hospital.

25

APPROACH YOUR WORK
AS AN ART FORM

Work brilliantly

Pablo Picasso was a brilliant artist and a fabulous businessman. He knew the value of his work. He loved to tell the story of a visitor to his studio who stood in front of a painting and asked, "What does it represent?" "Two hundred thousand dollars," Picasso replied. Picasso obviously viewed his art as a business, which it was.

Although I'll never be mistaken for Picasso, I always try to be an artist when I work. That means that I try to perform on the highest level. I view my business as an art, which it is. You should view your work that way, too.

Perform your work on the highest level and don't be afraid to ask to be paid what you're worth. Create goods or service that you're proud of and can stand behind. Think of your business as

INSIST ON PERFECTION

When I was building Trump Tower, I spent a great deal of time trying to find the exact color marble I wanted for the lobby. I looked at hundreds of samples until I found Breccia Perniche, a rare and very expensive marble. The color was a spectacular blend of rose, peach, and pink that was absolutely perfect.

I flew to the quarry in Italy to see the magnificent marble and I examined every bit of its huge supply. As I did, I noticed white spots and veins in most of the Breccia Perniche that detracted from its beauty. Nevertheless, I was determined to use this marble. So we marked off the best, most flawless slabs and scrapped the rest—about 60 percent of the total. It wasn't cost-effective, but it was worth it. The lobby in Trump Tower is truly a work of art, and the marble made the difference. It's gorgeous.

Trump Tower Atrium.
Photo courtesy of the Trump Organization.

your canvass. Become a master by constantly striving for excellence and not accepting less. When you establish yourself as a true artist, people will flock to you; they will beat down your door to know you, be your friend, and do business with you. Plus, it will make you feel great.

Artists are known for their dedication to their ideals and standards and for working to get their art exactly right. A recently discovered Beethoven manuscript was filled with cross outs, erasures, and changes, some of which punctured the pages. Although this manuscript was written toward the end of Beethoven's life, when he wasn't a music-writing novice, he was still a perfectionist who wouldn't settle for less than his best. He didn't need to impress anyone other than himself, but he kept correcting his work to improve it.

Top Yourself

Try to surpass your previous accomplishments. The most successful entrepreneurs compete with themselves to be the best they can be. They know that competing with others could lower their own standards.

Have your own vision and stick with it. Picasso definitely had his own way of seeing things, which worked to his advantage both artistically and financially. Don't be afraid to be unique. It's like being afraid of your best self.

In business, negotiating and making deals require a lot of background work. People don't see me doing that work, but it doesn't mean I don't do it. When people see the fabulous marble in Trump Tower, they have no idea what I went through to get the right end result just as they don't know what Picasso went through to make great art. Most people don't care about the blood, sweat, and tears that art or beauty requires; they care only about the results.

My work as a builder combines both craftsmanship and art because I refuse to settle for less. When I say I view my work as an art form, you can bet that I'm as meticulous as any artist would be about the materials and getting the results I want. If you do the same, I think you'll surprise yourself at how high your standards will become.

I've worked hard to make sure the Trump name is only on projects of the highest caliber and the finest quality. I won't approve anything that isn't the top of the line because when people see or hear "Trump," they expect the best. That's just basic marketing and good business.

—Donald J. Trump

 MAKE IT HAPPEN IN YOUR LIFE

Set your standards high and go about achieving them diligently. Be self-reliant and adhere to your own vision.

- Study the best people in your field and learn from them. Examine their approaches and styles and determine why they are unique.

- Identify what you can take from the masters and incorporate in your work, and then try to add your own personal twist. Stay within yourself, and don't be a pale imitation of someone else.

- Recognize your shortcomings. Learn where you need more knowledge, training, and experience. Then find out where and how to get it.

- Explore developments and breakthroughs in other fields to see if you could use them, or parts of them, in your work.

BEWARE

Approaching your work artistically can be bad business if you ignore the bottom line. If you focus too much attention on making every detail absolutely perfect, it may not be time- or cost-effective. Work artistically, but monitor your time, effort, and costs. Find the right balance without breaking the bank.

Sometimes you may exceed what the market requires and not get your price. But setting a high standard pays off in the long run and is always an asset, no matter what business you're in.

26

KEEP YOUR MIND IN THE GAME

Pay attention and stay focused

I often feel that my main job is problem solving. Many people perform well in trouble-free situations, but when problems arise, it's a different story. They can't solve problems, which I think is the key to running a successful business.

All businesses have problems. If you think that your business has no problems, then you're blind, pretending, or in denial. Maybe you don't operate your own business yet, but problems come with the territory. Expect problems to arise and never be surprised by them.

No matter how carefully you plan, how well you anticipate, or how hard you work, problems will occur. Events will take place and situations will arise that are simply beyond your control. And they happen suddenly, without warning. That's reality; that's how it works.

Early morning September 11, 2001, was a sunny, beautiful day in New York City. It held the promise of being a magnificent, late-summer day. Then disaster struck. Within two short hours, our feelings about that morning drastically changed.

September 11 is an extreme example, but I'm sure you see my point. Problems arise in a flash. Although we can't anticipate every possible development, it helps to plan for those you can. If you act, you may have a fighting chance to avoid or reduce the damage that will occur.

TAKE RESPONSIBILITY

Pay attention to your business; keep your mind in the game. Oversee your business and identify its strong points and weaknesses. Monitor your people's performance and determine who should be doing what. Find out what problems exist and anticipate those that are likely to arise. Nip problems in the bud before they grow into more serious and hard-to-solve issues.

In other words, take responsibility. People who take responsibility have no need to blame or continually find fault with others. Naysayers rarely contribute much, and they usually don't amount to much.

> Don't find a fault, find a remedy.
>
> —Henry Ford

By now, I've been in business long enough to have had ups and downs. I've enjoyed magnificent victories and suffered

INSIST ON PERFECTION

A guy used to constantly call me and complain about everybody and their brother. To listen to him you would think that the entire world was against him and that he never made a mistake in his life. From day one, nothing was ever his fault; everyone else was to blame. In truth, he was his own biggest blind spot, and, sad to say, he eventually became a total loser because he never remedied his biggest problem—himself.

When things go wrong, look at yourself first. Don't instinctively blame others or the circumstances—or use them to cover your behind. Be the leader; stand tall, and take the hit. If you accept the glory, be willing to accept blame.

painful defeats. I've learned to go quickly from seeing problems to seeing their solutions. The secret to resolving problems is to emphasize the solution more than the problem; accentuate the positive without ignoring the negative.

And here's another tip for those of you who work for others— even if you plan to venture out on your own. Learn to be invaluable team players. You may have noticed on *The Apprentice* that the people who lack strong team skills don't do as well. Although each candidate on the show wants to win, a critical part of the contest is to work well on teams. In any business, at any level, being a good team player is crucial. Master how to be a team player because it really pays.

Unfortunately, I've noticed how often *The Apprentice* candidates bicker and fight, which wastes precious time, is annoying, and can be embarrassing. To see and hear such bright, highly qualified individuals carrying on, frequently over the most inconsequential stuff, shows that they haven't heeded Henry Ford's advice to find a remedy rather than a fault.

 COACH TRUMP MAKE IT HAPPEN IN YOUR LIFE

Here are some tips for keeping your mind in the game:

- Eliminate all distractions and give your full attention to your work. I'm constantly surprised at how easily people lose focus and don't pay enough attention. At work, it's your job to know what's going on.

- Understand that problems will occur, and some will be beyond your control. Concentrate on those you can control, and find people who can resolve the others.

- Take responsibility, and don't just lash out at others. Focus on solving problems. As a leader, be willing to accept responsibility for problems and failures as well as praise for triumphs.

Ask Mr. Trump: Questions from Readers of the Trump University Blog

Q: I make many business decisions, but I often question myself and feel anxious about my choices. This often leads to procrastination. How can I overcome these obstacles?

DJT: It's good to question yourself before making decisions. Make sure you cover everything you can and are thorough. Understand that this approach can cause anxiety, which is natural, but after a while, your instincts will sharpen and you will become more confident about your decisions. Experience builds confidence, but being thorough to begin with will alleviate lots of your anxiety.

If your anxiety continues, give yourself deadlines. Deadlines produce order; they force you to be more organized and responsible.

27

It Takes Courage
to Persist

Business pressures never stop

Courage is a frequently misunderstood concept. When most people hear the word, they think of heroism during war or disasters such as earthquakes, floods, and other calamities. Courage is equated with superhero-level bravery, against overwhelming odds, and feats that are far beyond most of our capabilities.

I think of the word *courage* differently. Yes, it applies to heroic actions, but it also means working day after day, year after year, without becoming discouraged, worn down, or bitter. It means persisting, carrying on without letting up, and consistently giving your best.

Courage isn't the absence of fear; it's the conquering of fear. Just because people appear confident doesn't mean that they are not afraid. Many great performers suffer stage fright and must fight to overcome it. With some, the fear never goes away, but they still perform and do so brilliantly. They work through their fears to persist and overcome. They know that their job is to go on stage and perform regardless of how they feel. To be a star, to succeed, talent alone isn't enough; success takes work and requires courage.

Courage is grace under pressure.

—Ernest Hemingway

Business Never Stops

Business never stops; it keeps moving on—you can't rest on your laurels or become complacent. If you stop or relax, you may put yourself out of business because someone is always eager to take your place. To survive, you must be determined, persistent, and prepared for the long run—even when the odds are stacked against you. That's where courage comes in.

People are surprised to learn that I put in 12-hour working days. For me, that's the norm, not the exception. To remain successful, I have to be persistent and work hard; I work long hours to get everything done. If you usually work a 40-hour week and then add on another 20 hours a week for a few weeks, you'll be surprised at how much more you can accomplish. Productive people accomplish more for a reason—they work long and hard.

Michelangelo was a tenacious genius who went to extremes for his art. And his results were spectacular. He had to be courageous to succeed during a tumultuous time in history in which he dealt with the Medici family, a variety of popes, warring families, and Girolamo Savonarola—famous for burning artistic works. Michelangelo often worked in appalling conditions and under demanding, dictatorial, unreasonable people, but he consistently created magnificent art. To reach such heights took persistence and courage as great as his talent. Although few of us know the names of other figures from the sixteenth century, most of us know about Michelangelo. That's real staying power.

The candidates on *The Apprentice* are courageous. They had to survive interviews, auditions, and intense competition. Over a million people apply each year to be on the show. In the face of those odds, the candidates who are selected had to be persistent. This demonstrates that we've had no losers on the show. Everyone who appeared on the program has been a winner.

No one wants to be rejected, especially on television in front of millions of people. So being a candidate on *The Apprentice* takes guts, real courage, and I give each participant a great deal of credit. I know that they will all succeed, whether they are chosen as my apprentice or not.

I can be hard on people when I believe they can do more and I don't feel that they have been living up to their potential. I may have more faith in their abilities than they do; I may be the catalyst that gets them going.

A young executive was in my office when I learned I wouldn't be able to make a speaking engagement. When I told him he would have to step in for me, he said, "Oh, I don't do public speaking." "You do now!" I replied. And do you know what? He spoke, and he was terrific. And he has now become an accomplished public speaker. That young man just needed a nudge—well, maybe a shove—to get going. I need people who can think—and speak—on their feet, and that's one way to develop them.

 **COACH TRUMP** MAKE IT HAPPEN IN YOUR LIFE

Teach yourself to become more courageous by following these tips:

- Identify your goals. Know precisely what you want to achieve, and then plan the best route for success.

- Be determined, and continue despite the obstacles you face. Persistence is essential in achieving success.

- Address your fears. If your fears are realistic, find a way to overcome them. Get more training, more experience, or put in more hours and work harder.

28

JOIN THE EXPLORERS' CLUB

Learn about the mysteries of life

Emerson said, "Do not go where the path may lead; go instead where there is no path and leave a trail." I've followed that advice and recommended it. You won't be successful by following someone else's route. So spend some time focusing on your own path and your own purpose. Take off your training wheels.

Although I'm always busy, I set aside a quiet time every morning and every evening. I need it to keep my equilibrium and stay centered on my own path. It recharges my batteries, lets me unwind, and helps me refocus on my major goals. I don't like being swayed by anything that might be negative or damaging.

Life is a series of discoveries that helps us learn and grow. Albert Einstein observed that, "The mind that opens to a new idea never comes back to its original size." I agree. Once children learn to walk, they don't want to go back and crawl; they want to get up off the ground, stand up, and move forward. We have a responsibility to ourselves to keep moving forward, do our best, and try to live up to our potential.

When you break it down, it's pretty simple because all we have to do is tune in to our talents and capabilities. I didn't say it was easy; I said it was simple. There are plenty of obstacles, and we may fall a lot before we actually walk. It's also easy to get so distracted that you don't tune in. Since we're continually bombarded by information and relentless demands, it's a challenge to find quiet time when we can hear our own thoughts and decipher the flood of information we constantly receive. We must unplug before we can plug back in.

Donald J. Trump at his New York City apartment.
Photo courtesy of the Trump Organization.

THINK FOR YOURSELF

When people don't think for themselves, problems occur. In fact, the lowest points in history occurred when people stopped thinking for themselves and followed the wrong individuals. These times gave rise to dictators; genocide; and brutal, inhuman behavior.

Identify your *intrinsic values*—what you really want and are willing to work hard to get. They provide you with strength, determination, and a powerful compass. Look at the big picture; think on a *Trump scale*. Find out what you really want to dedicate your life to and then go out and achieve it.

Follow your own path because it will bring you to the places you were meant to be.

—Donald J. Trump

For me, life is all about discovery. I feel best when I learn something I didn't know. Although I work in a reality-based business, I have a strong respect for the mysteries of life because they make me feel like an explorer on an exciting quest. They heighten my natural curiosity, making me constantly question and want to learn more. As a result, I'm introduced to amazing people, and my life is constantly enriched with new understandings, insights, and knowledge. Don't put blinders on or limit yourself; reach out, seek, and explore.

The Apprentice was a new challenge and discovery for me. It brought out the educator in me. It showed me how much I love to teach and see people develop and grow. It has been marvelous to watch the program's candidates develop as they tackle new experiences and discover more and more each week.

Trump University has been a natural progression from *The Apprentice*, and it's giving me the opportunity to educate on a much larger scale. Both of these experiences have been exciting discoveries that make me thirst for more; I can't wait to see what I'll become involved in next!

Finding your purpose may take a while or all of your life. Or you could have discovered it when you were five years old and are still refining it. Since we all differ and have varying priorities, we all must move at our own pace. Make it a priority to keep exploring, learning, discovering, and moving forward because that is the best recipe for a successful life.

A Very Special Week (Plus) in My Life: A New Baby!

Monday

In the early morning of March 20, 2006, our beautiful baby boy was born! What a wonderful feeling! We named him Barron William Trump.

Featured on the Cover of *People* Magazine. Photo courtesy of the Trump Organization.

I was scheduled to be a guest on Don Imus's radio show that morning, but I completely forgot, which is understandable, considering the circumstances. However, Don didn't know the circumstances, and he wasn't too pleased about my no-show. I got a message from Rhona that he was mad, so I called him to share the first public announcement of our son's birth. Don's been a friend for years, so I was pleased to make the announcement on his show.

A Very Special Week (Plus) in My Life: A New Baby!

Tuesday

I carried on the day-to-day business at the Trump Organization, and I was scheduled to do a live call-in to *Larry King*. Today had a celebratory buzz to it, and

we received an unbelievable number of gifts for Barron, including a baby carriage with a built-in chandelier from Ellen DeGeneres.

I'd like to thank everyone for their gifts and their cards, we got many from very kind fans, and it would be impossible to acknowledge every one of them.

Baby Carriage for Barron Trump Given by Ellen DeGeneres. Photo courtesy of the Trump Organization.

A Very Special Week (Plus) in My Life: A New Baby!

Wednesday

8:30 A.M. I make and take some phone calls, and have meetings with Bernie Diamond, Jill Cremer, Andy Weiss, and Cathy Glosser.

9:45 A.M. I pick up Melania and Barron William from the hospital and take them home. The nursery is ready and having our new addition makes everything seem even better. I spend some time at home and then go back down to the office to . . . well, see Monday, Tuesday, and Wednesday of last week for a general idea. As you can see, running the Trump Organization is anything but boring. They even fixed the copy machine. Things are looking up.

29

CONFIDENCE IS A MAGNET

It will draw people to you

Many factors affect whether you seize opportunities, and I think most begin with self-confidence. Believing in yourself can take you where you want to go, but uncertainty can destroy your chances of success. When you feel good about yourself and are convinced about your talents and abilities, everything is easier and more fun. Other people will respond to you, believe in you, and help you reach your goals. You'll have that "top of the world" feeling and feed off the energy it provides.

Never let anyone undermine your confidence, especially yourself. Know your business expertly and in depth. Always be totally prepared so that doubters, disbelievers, and competitors can't throw you off track. People like winners, so project that you are one. People want to know, transact business with, and be friends with winners. Your self-assurance can transform people's doubts and fears, eliminate negativity, and help you attain greater success.

Even if you haven't yet enjoyed great success, keep working to master your field. Become an expert and an authority. Keep working and learning because the more you learn, the more self-confidence you will gain.

Confidence is a magnet that will draw people to you and make your life—and theirs—a lot more pleasant.

—Donald J. Trump

When I first began to work in Manhattan, I had to be courageous because I had entered a new territory that was not my home turf. I was literally the new kid on the block who had much to learn. I did my homework, studied hard, and closely watched what was going on, but I was still paving my way and trying to figure it all out.

I knew that I had to appear confident or I'd never be taken seriously. And I've never lost that edge. I knew I was in the big time, playing with the biggest, brightest, and best businesspeople. If I was going to operate on their level, I had to show my competitors that I had what it took to win.

I still feel that way and try to project that confidence. That is one reason I've been able to achieve so much. You can do the same, regardless of where you are now. Know where you want to go, prepare and believe in yourself, and you'll get there.

SHOW DISCERNMENT

If you really want to succeed in business, you have to work at it every day. I do. The big time isn't for slackers. When you work at it, an amazing thing occurs: You accumulate an incredible body of knowledge in your area of expertise and develop the uncanny ability to make the right calls consistently. Getting to this level is an awesome achievement; it's the essence of success. It's why so many successful people never want to retire or stop what they do so well. More than the money, acclaim, and success, experts hate to give up the mastery of their business. That mastery is what makes them special and separates them from the pack.

Working at your business every day also builds up the strength and stamina it takes to carry heavy loads. In the long run, confidence will prove invaluable and give you a decided edge over others who are as well prepared.

 MAKE IT HAPPEN IN YOUR LIFE

Here are some suggestions for building self-confidence:

- Learn your area of expertise fully, in great detail, so that you become a leader in your field. Become the best at what you do; it will improve your business and your life.

- Let your actions show that you're the best. See each day as an opportunity to show that you can do business at the highest level.

30

Keep Your Momentum Rolling

But never lose control

When you're putting together a deal, you often develop great momentum. All of the pieces fall neatly in place and come together seamlessly. You feel energized, indomitable, and everything seems easy and fun. But that momentum can lull you into a false sense of security because your momentum can vanish quickly if you don't work to maintain it.

MOMENTUM

When I use the word *momentum*, I mean the powerful burst of energy that creates force, strength, and impetus to drive you forward. Working fast also helps me build the stamina to maintain and strengthen my pace.

I'll never be a wallflower—I'd rather build walls than cling to them.

—Donald J. Trump

The first thing to understand about momentum is that it exists. You can't take full advantage of this vital energy if you don't know it's there. Learn to recognize it and, once you can, let it sweep you forward. Use its force to propel you, but maintain your course.

A hugely successful real estate developer, who I admired, was going thorough a steep and unfortunate business decline. When we met at a party, I asked him what brought on his hard times. "Donald," he said, "I lost my momentum, and I couldn't get it back."

His response haunted me and taught me a great lesson. I began to study momentum and learned what a potent force it could be. Since then, I've continued studying the power of momentum and I apply it to my life and business. I never want to lose my momentum and slide, so I consciously think about my momentum; I monitor it, and work hard to keep it going.

INERTIA

Inertia is the opposite of momentum. It holds you down and traps you. When you sense the onset of inertia, fight back. Treat it like negative thinking and zap it at its first appearance. Don't let inertia hold you back because it can be murder to shake.

People frequently lose momentum by getting in their own way. I knew a man who always took 10 big, fast steps forward and

INSIST ON PERFECTION

In the late 1980s, a *Newsweek* ad (September 28, 1987) featured a photograph of me with the caption "Few things in life are as brash as *Newsweek*." I don't mind being called brash because to me it's the same as saying I'm bold, have energy, and get things done. However, brashness can also imply acting without constraint, which definitely isn't me. I firmly believe in constraints and I diligently monitor and try to control my momentum. So I don't really consider myself to be brash, but I prefer it to being too timid.

then sat back as if he had reached a plateau. When he stopped and relaxed, he was usually overtaken by someone else. Yet he continued to follow the identical pattern. He acted as if all he had to do was put his plans in motion, work like mad for a while to prime the pump, and then sit back and watch his profits perpetually flow. Instead of capitalizing on his momentum, he stopped. He was caught in his own inertia.

 MAKE IT HAPPEN IN YOUR LIFE

Energy is the key to accomplishment. Harness your energy and you will have the ability to achieve your goals.

- Develop the ability to sense when you're on a roll, which usually happens when you have extra energy that improves your performance.

- Let your momentum carry you. Hook into it, feel the power of your momentum, and let it sweep you along.

- As your momentum carries you, stay in control. Watch out for hazards and make sure that you keep moving in the right direction.

Ask Mr. Trump: Questions from Readers of the Trump University Blog

Q: I'm $500,000 in debt. I've been told to give up and file for bankruptcy, but the business, aside from the old debt, is profitable and sales are increasing. I'm feeling a little defeated. How can I get my focus back?

DJT: Focus on the solution to your problems. If you dwell only on the problems, you might miss opportunities that could move your momentum in the right direction. Problems can be solved; sometimes problems lead us to bigger and better things. Be realistic, but remain optimistic. Negativity will kill your chances of gaining momentum. Instead, focus on the possibilities and don't give up.

31

Is the Problem a Blip or a Catastrophe?

Expect problems and keep moving forward

Early in my real estate career as I was putting a deal together, I thought I'd worked through every possible obstacle. Boy was I wrong. No sooner would I solve a problem than several more would immediately pop up. It took me months of hammering away at details to complete that deal. Had I known from the beginning what I would have to go through, I'm not sure I would have become involved. However, in retrospect, I'm glad I did. That problem-filled project was my first big success—the development of the Grand Hyatt Hotel in New York City. I got the equivalent of several PhDs from that deal.

How we handle adversity says a lot about who we are. Situations that destroy some people enable others to thrive. Since problems always arise, it's essential to know how to deal with them.

When many people encounter obstacles, they go into shock, become paralyzed, and freeze. They don't know what to do, so they do nothing or react impulsively without thinking and make poor decisions.

Brilliant business operators take problems and turn them into gold.

—Donald J. Trump

When difficulties occur, I always ask, "Is this a blip or a catastrophe? Is it a minor annoyance or a serious problem?" The answer helps me focus and find the best way to proceed.

Here's how to handle problems and setbacks:

- Step back and examine the issue; get a more objective and less emotional picture of the situation. Give yourself room to see more clearly and think. Assess the problem from all angles, with an open mind, and you'll usually find its cause. Try not to make assumptions because they frequently lead to mistakes.
- Address the situation. List the solutions you can take to minimize the damage quickly, efficiently, cost-effectively, and permanently. Consider and evaluate all of your options. Keep in mind that "When one door closes, another door opens." Other alternatives will usually exist, but you have to find them. Many people stare at open doors and don't see that they're open, let alone realize their significance.

Being $9 billion in debt taught me to maintain my focus and momentum at all times. That was an expensive lesson! And at that steep price, I either had to learn or go out of business; so I learned—a great deal.

I discovered that I had allowed myself to be diverted. I had loosened my grip and relaxed my control. I lost my focus and before I knew it, I was facing my worst nightmare. As soon as I seemed vulnerable, everyone piled on. I had to get out from under all my problems and find some room to breathe. So I returned to the basics, focused on my business, and discovered what went wrong. I pulled back, analyzed my mistakes, and learned from them so that I could move forward.

Expect Problems

I always expect problems. Rarely is anything that's worth doing problem free. Sometimes I feel like Sisyphus, condemned to push a boulder uphill for eternity. I just keep pushing, shoulder to boulder, moving forward; I don't give up. My focus is intense, and I've learned from demanding situations that have made me strong.

You also have to learn when to quit and when to move forward. This can be tricky because a fine line frequently exists between acceptance and resignation. Since everyone makes mistakes, try to be understanding when other people fail. Don't immediately give up on them; you wouldn't want others to write you off without a fair chance. The fine line widens when you find out that someone is a scoundrel or incompetent and will never change. When that's the case, break off the relationship, cut your losses, and eliminate that person from your life.

 MAKE IT HAPPEN IN YOUR LIFE

When problems arise, try these tips:

- Understand that difficulties, mistakes, and setbacks are an inevitable part of business and life. No matter how well you plan and how hard you work, things can always change and require you to react.

- Dealing with trouble promptly is usually the best approach and is generally more cost-effective than hoping trouble will go away.

- Don't allow problems to knock you off your feet. Take sufficient time to determine the problem's cause, and then deal with it objectively and reasonably. Get expert advice.

- Learn from each situation. As you deal with each problem, note what you learned from it so you don't repeat that same mistake. Situations often repeat themselves, so next time the problem occurs, you should be prepared to handle it.

32

REACH WITHIN TO
RISE ABOVE

But temper your reach with reality

A fter they reach a goal, achievers don't feel that they've reached a plateau; they think they're just beginning. Achievers have motors that drive them forward at all times; they don't have neutral or reverse. Achievers always look for the next deal and have another objective or venture to pursue. An achiever's enthusiasm isn't fabricated; it comes from deep within. Achievers thrive on challenges, and they see every deal as another opportunity to surpass themselves and accomplish even more.

Look deeply within yourself to discover your higher self—the essential you. Find out what you really want, what you truly value, and how far you'll go to get it. In the process, you'll also find out what you're made of.

One night at 3:00 A.M., when I was more than $9 billion in debt, I was summoned to Citibank for a conference call with a bevy of international bankers to whom I owed money. It was raining like a monsoon, and I couldn't get a cab. I had to walk 15 blocks to the bank, and I felt like I was sloshing my way to the guillotine.

When I arrived, I was soaked. I felt like I had reached my lowest point. It would have been so easy to throw in the towel and return home to my dry, warm, comfortable bed, but something inside me couldn't quit.

So I remained and braced myself to take their best shots. As the call proceeded, I dug down deep and focused on what I needed to do. My juices began flowing, my focus sharpened, and I fought back. Soaked, exhausted, and massively deep in debt, I hung in there and didn't quit.

We worked things out, and, as they say, the rest is history. You know what I say—never, ever give up.

Your higher self continually needs to be fed so it can grow. That part of you must constantly strive to build a productive, fulfilling life that is rich in the things that are most essential to you, which doesn't necessarily mean money.

When we understand our higher selves, it can help us become more visionary. Unfortunately, the word *visionary* may evoke a negative image such as being a castle builder or a Don Quixote—someone with unrealistic dreams. However, it's fine to be a dreamer provided you're also realistic. Visionaries move the world and create new dimensions. Look at Bill Gates in technology and Mark Burnett in reality television or Pablo Picasso, Igor Stravinsky, and other great artists. Each followed his vision and enriched the world.

An achievement is a bondage. It obliges one to a higher achievement.

—Albert Camus

Allow Mistakes

Despite all that Thomas Alva Edison accomplished, he continually searched to make new and more important discoveries. His outlook toward the discovery process is best illustrated by his statement, "I haven't failed; I just found 10,000 ways that don't work." Edison knew the value of constantly trying. He also understood that trying was more important than the mistakes he might make because the easiest way to avoid mistakes is not to try.

However, mistakes are part of the process; you can't learn without them. So allow yourself to make mistakes. I don't mean that you should be sloppy or not care when you err. I mean that trying is what counts, making the attempt.

When you make mistakes, learn from them. Ask yourself what lesson you learned from each mistake. If you keep learning, you will move closer to your goals.

Our goals can be elusive. We may only have a feeling or an inkling that something great will happen, but we don't precisely know what it will be. At that point, we can either block it out or move forward and hope that our vision will become clearer.

I keep working. I focus my energy on the projects I need to address, and the right answers often come to me. Taking my mind off the problem, changing my focus, and reducing the pressure also help the solutions appear.

 Make It Happen in Your Life

- Don't just agree to the wishes of others or do what they say you should.

- Trust your feelings. Your inner feelings have a way of telling you what's right for you. They are your personal warning system and most trusted advisor, so listen to them.

- Assemble a group of trusted advisors with whom you can discuss sticky problems. Select people who have good judgment, wide experience, diverse talents, and expertise in areas in which you may be weak and who care about you.

- Consider your advisors' advice, but make your own decisions. Only you know what's right for you, and you will have to live with the impact of your decisions.

33

CONCENTRATE ON THE TARGET, NOT ON THE WEAPON

Focus on what matters most

Viewers of *The Apprentice* were shocked when I fired four candidates in one episode. I took this drastic and unprecedented step because I was disgusted with their performance on a sales task and couldn't decide who among them did the worst job. So they all crammed into a taxi for the final ride home.

In that episode, the Excel team lost their focus. Its members spent most of their time creating a remarkable presentation that shoppers loved. So much so, that they spent all of their time at the batting cage and didn't buy goods. Although Excel created a popular attraction, what good did it do? It didn't increase sales; in fact, store sales decreased. Excel missed the boat by forgetting the task's overall objective.

INSIST ON PERFECTION

The teams' task was straightforward: create an interactive sales event in a sporting goods store. The team making the most sales would win. The members of Excel created an elaborate batting cage. It wowed shoppers who waited in long lines to try it. The team members worked the pitching machine and gave hitting tips while they hawked hot dogs and lemonade. They were so caught up in the excitement of the event that they forgot the main goal—sell the store's merchandise.

Meanwhile, the other team, Capital Edge constructed a mini putting green for the shoppers' children. The putting green occupied the kids while their parents shopped in the store. Capital Edge produced a 74 percent increase in store sales while Excel had a 34 percent drop, the biggest loss in the history of *The Apprentice*. Capital Edge's win was a no-brainer.

STYLE OVER SUBSTANCE

It's amazing how often I see the same basic mistake. Extremely bright and capable people get so involved in glittery, eye-catching pitches and other less important matters that they ignore the bottom line. They lose their focus.

I get invited to lots of lavish events. While these events can be dazzling, exciting, and terrific fun, I frequently wonder how effective they actually are. In most cases, the ideas and execution are great, often brilliant. Yet just as often, they don't generate big sales, which is really what counts.

We all love inventive ideas, fabulous events, and beautiful things, and I try to always have them in my life. However, when it comes to business, they are just a means to the end. Events, advertising, and promotions are not ends in and of themselves. They exist to attract people's attention and increase sales. Even if they help you get your foot in the door, or into a conference room, you still have to close the deal and make the sale.

It's easy to lose focus. Things come wrapped in the most attractive, alluring packages. Many may take your breath away, but don't let them. Zone in on what matters most and try to *excel*. Don't be diverted; instead, stay focused on what matters most or you could be *expelled*.

Ask Mr. Trump: Questions from Readers of the Trump University Blog

Q: What is the best way to coach members of your sales force who consistently don't reach their sales goals, but who have excellent personal qualities and work habits.

DJT: Business is about making money; businesses need income to stay alive. It may sound simplistic, but it's a fact. Make it clear to your salespeople that if they don't close sales, your business can't stay afloat, and they'll lose their jobs. Stress the importance of their productivity to your company's success. Point out their strengths and encourage them to build on them. If they still don't meet your sales goals, they may not be right for the job. Some terrific people have a talent for sales and some don't. See if their strengths would be better suited in other parts of your organization.

I had a sales associate who showed a greater aptitude for property development than he did for sales. So we moved him to our project management team where he has become very valuable. When employees have great traits, but aren't succeeding, look for the hidden talents and areas where they could thrive.

Appendix A

The Trump Organization at a Glance

Property Portfolio

New York

Trump Tower

Trump Park Avenue

Trump World Tower

Trump International
    Hotel & Tower

Trump Palace

The Residences at Trump
    National

Trump Parc & Trump
    Parc East

Trump Place

610 Park Avenue

40 Wall Street

Trump Tower at Westchester

Los Angeles

The Estates at Trump National

Chicago

Trump International Hotel & Tower

Florida

Trump International Hotel
& Tower

Trump Towers

Trump Las Olas Beach Resort

Trump Hollywood

Trump Tower Tampa

Trump Grande

The Mar-a-Lago Club

Las Vegas

Trump International Hotel & Tower

Canouan Island, the Grenadines

Trump Island Villas

Seoul, Korea

Trump World

Toronto, Canada

Trump International Hotel & Tower

Future Developments

Honolulu, Hawaii

New Orleans, Louisiana

Jersey City, New Jersey

Westchester, New York

Sao Paolo, Brazil

Dubai, United Arab Emirates

Panama City, Panama, Trump
Ocean Club

Sales & Mortgage

Trump Sales & Leasing (Residential Sales & Leasing)

Trump Mortgage

Golf Clubs

Trump National Golf Club, Los Angeles, California
Trump National Golf Club, Bedminster, New Jersey
Trump National Golf Club, Westchester, New York
Trump International Golf Club, West Palm Beach, Florida
Trump International Golf Club, Canouan Island, the Grenadines
Aberdeen Golf Club, Scotland

Casino Resorts

Trump Taj Mahal Casino Resort, Atlantic City, New Jersey
Trump Plaza Hotel & Casino, Atlantic City, New Jersey
Trump Marina Hotel Casino, Atlantic City, New Jersey
Trump Club Privee, Canouan Island, the Grenadines

Entertainment

The Apprentice
Trumped: The Radio Show
Trump Model Management
Trump Pageants
Miss Universe   *Miss USA*   *Miss Teen USA*

Wollman and Lasker Skating Rinks

TRUMP UNIVERSITY: COURSES OFFERED

Real Estate

Entrepreneurship

Management

Wealth Creation

MERCHANDISE

Signature Collection

Men's suits

Neckwear

Dress shirts

Cuff links

Small leather goods

Eyewear

Sportswear

Timepieces

Books

Trump: The Art of the Deal

Trump: Think Like a Billionaire

Trump: The Way to the Top

Trump: How to Get Rich

Trump 101: The Way to Success

Trump: The Best Golf Advice I Ever Received

Trump: The Best Real Estate Advice I Ever Received

The America We Deserve

The Art of the Comeback

Men's Fragrance

Trump: The Fragrance

Trump Ice

Naturally pure spring water

TRAVEL

GoTrump.com, Travel Trump Style

A full-service travel agency

TRUMP FOOD AND RESTAURANTS

Trump Buffet

Trump Ice Cream Parlor

Trump Bar

Trump Tower Grill

Trump Catering

Appendix B

The Trump Store

Ten Books I Recommend You Read

Think Like a Billionaire: Everything You Need to Know about Success, Real Estate and Life by Donald J. Trump and Meredith McIver (Random House, 2005).

Trump: The Art of the Deal by Donald J. Trump and Tony Schwartz (Random House, 1987).

The Art of War: The Oldest Military Treatise in the World by Sun-Tzu (Dover Publications, 2002).

The Prince by Niccolo Machiavelli (Bantam Classics, 1984).

What It Takes to Be #1: Vince Lombardi on Leadership by Vince Lombardi (McGraw-Hill, 2001).

The Power of Positive Thinking by Norman Vincent Peale (Prentice-Hall, 1952).

Iacocca: An Autobiography by Lee Iacocca and William Novak (Bantam Books, 1984).

Cashflow Quadrant: Rich Dad's Guide to Financial Freedom by Robert T. Kiyosaki and Sharon L. Lechter (Warner Business Books, 2000).

10 Clowns Don't Make a Circus: And 249 Other Critical Management Success Strategies by Steven Schragis and Rick Frishman (Adams Media Corp., 2006).

Rich Woman: A Book on Investing for Women—Because I Hate Being Told What to Do by Kim Kiyosaki (Rich Press, 2006).

INDEX